T R

The mental

C000213930

www.triggerp

The**inspirational**series™
Overcoming adversity and thriving

Lost Boy Found
Redrawing the Lines of my Life

BY ANDREW PUCCETTI

We are proud to introduce The**inspirational**series™. Part of the Trigger family of innovative mental health books, The**inspirational**series™ tells the stories of the people who have battled and beaten mental health issues. For more information visit: www.triggerpublishing.com

THE AUTHOR

 Andrew Puccetti is a college student, activist, and mental illness survivor. After being diagnosed with multiple mental illnesses and hitting rock bottom, Andrew managed to change his life for the better. He now lives a happy, fulfilling life and is passionate about sharing his story so that others know what it feels like to live in the shoes of someone who suffers with mental illness. He hopes to bring more understanding to others, help people know they are not alone in their struggles, and break the stigma around such issues.

Andrew lives in the suburbs of Chicago, Illinois with his family and two dogs. Outside of writing, he enjoys eating delicious vegetarian food, spending time with the people he loves, and seeing as many musical theater productions as he possibly can. You can find out more about Andrew on his website at www.andrewpuccettiauthor.com.

First published in Great Britain 2019 by Trigger

Trigger is a trading style of Shaw Callaghan Ltd & Shaw Callaghan 23 USA, INC.

The Foundation Centre

Navigation House, 48 Millgate, Newark

Nottinghamshire NG24 4TS UK

www.triggerpublishing.com

Copyright © Andrew Puccetti 2019

British Library Cataloguing in Publication Data

A CIP catalogue record for this book is available upon request
from the British Library

ISBN: 9781912478347

This book is also available in the following e-Book and Audio formats:

MOBI: 9781912478378
EPUB: 9781912478354
PDF: 9781912478361

Andrew Puccetti has asserted his right under the Copyright,
Design and Patents Act 1988 to be identified as the author of this work

Typeset by Fusion Graphic Design Ltd

Printed and bound in Great Britain by Clays Ltd, Elcograf S.p.A

Paper from responsible sources

TRIGGER™
The mental health & wellbeing publisher

www.triggerpublishing.com

Thank you for purchasing this book.
You are making an incredible difference.

Proceeds from all Trigger books go directly to
The Shaw Mind Foundation, a global charity that focuses
entirely on mental health. To find out more about
The Shaw Mind Foundation visit,
www.shawmindfoundation.org

MISSION STATEMENT

Our goal is to make help and support available for every
single person in society, from all walks of life.
We will never stop offering hope. These are our promises.

Trigger and The Shaw Mind Foundation

the *Shaw* mind
FOUNDATION

Creating hope for children,
adults and families

A NOTE FROM THE SERIES EDITOR

The Inspirational range from Trigger brings you genuine stories about our authors' experiences with mental health problems.

Some of the stories in our Inspirational range will move you to tears. Some will make you laugh. Some will make you feel angry, or surprised, or uplifted. Hopefully they will all change the way you see mental health problems.

These are stories we can all relate to and engage with. Stories of people experiencing mental health difficulties and finding their own ways to overcome them with dignity, humour, perseverance and spirit.

Andrew writes openly and honestly about his OCD, Borderline Personality Disorder, and depression, leading us through his life as these things threw him off the path he worked so hard to walk. Exploring what it means to be young and battling severe mental health problems, Andrew tells a fulfilling story of overcoming that which held him back, of living, not just surviving.

This is our Inspirational range. These are our stories. We hope you enjoy them. And most of all, we hope that they will educate and inspire you. That's what this range is all about.

Lauren Callaghan,
Co-founder and Lead Consultant Psychologist at Trigger

*To Mom and Dad. Thank you for loving me
even when I didn't love myself.*

Disclaimer: Some names and identifying details have been changed to protect the privacy of individuals.

Trigger Warning: This book contains references to suicidal thoughts.

Trigger encourages diversity and different viewpoints, and is dedicated to telling genuine stories of people's experiences of mental health issues. However, all views, thoughts, and opinions expressed in this book are the author's own, and are not necessarily representative of Trigger as an organisation.

HOW DID I GET HERE?

February 1, 2017.

I'm 20 years old. Alone in a rather plain-looking, dark room, with only two beds, two desks, and one armchair for furniture. The smell of disinfectant lingers in the air. I'm wearing nothing but a paper gown and a pair of hospital-issued socks that they gave to me when I was admitted.

I'm standing in front of the single window, looking out at the setting sun, tears streaming down my face.

A nurse peeks her head into the room without knocking, pushing open the door. I wasn't surprised; privacy no longer existed for me here. A nurse is always somewhere, checking on me every 10 minutes, leaving me with no peace.

I quickly wipe my eyes to hide the fact that I've just been crying, not that it would have been considered abnormal here. She asks me to come down the hallway so she can take my blood, and even though she asks, I know there is no choice, so I say yes, and she quietly leaves the room.

I stand there a second longer, watching the cars passing by, and I can't help but think about the people inside, about how they're going about their lives, not thinking about how lucky they are to be free. Free from a hospital, from a psych ward, from their own heads.

I guess that's what heaven might be like.

How did I get here?

I keep asking myself that, over and over again. On one hand, I am talking about the hospital, trying to piece together how I came to be here, but that isn't all of it. I want to know how my mind got here, how I got to no longer wanting to exist, no longer wanting to be part of the earth.

PART ONE

CHAPTER 1

I was born in the northwest suburbs of Chicago in November 1996 to Renee and Richard Puccetti. I was their firstborn, and the start of their new beginning living outside of the city. My parents were high-school sweethearts, and had lived their entire lives in the city. But after having me, they decided they wanted a quieter life for their newborn son and packed up, moving to the white-picket-fenced suburbs of Mount Prospect, Illinois.

All my mother ever wanted was a *Brady Bunch* life, telling herself that she would be a regular Carol Brady. Born in February of 1970, Mom was born to a young couple who had gotten married not too long before they had her. About a year later, my aunt was born. And about a year after that, her father, my grandfather, came out as gay and left his wife and two young children. As a result of her father leaving them, Mom grew up in poverty. Most of her childhood was seen moving from apartment to apartment, bounced from school to school. So it was no surprise that she wanted nothing more than the perfect life for her own children.

My father, my biggest role model, is a successful businessman and entrepreneur. Born in February 1969, he grew up in the city and had, what he calls, a 'classic Chicago childhood' of being barely supervised, playing nonstop, and staying out until dinner, and most often after that. When he was 17, his sister was shot and passed away, the effects of which are still felt in his family today. Despite how hard it was for them, they carried on, my father starting his first real job with a recruiting company, going from taking out the garbage to owning his own company, eventually becoming a leader in his industry. My father is a stubborn man, something that has often come up between us, but I see him as the best father in the world: kind, generous, and loving.

However, the first few years of my life, he suffered from alcoholism. From what I know, my father had been that way ever since he was a teenager. And he wasn't alone in that. Alcoholism has always run in my family, on both sides. Many of my relatives have met their demise from alcohol, and I believe that alcoholism can be genetic, etching its way from person to person. Fortunately, my dad's alcoholism didn't have too much of an effect on me, as I was too young to know anything, but it had a drastic effect on my mother.

Although he usually kept himself sober during the week, he was gone every weekend, coming home completely intoxicated. My parents fought all the time as a result, but my mom was determined not to get a divorce because she still loved him, so she plastered a smile on her face and took care of him for three long years. No one knew, not even the closest of friends and family. Mom became depressed, losing 50 pounds over the period of six months. She struggled to take care of me and just laid in bed crying all day. I think for a while, it felt like she could do nothing in the face of it all.

However, Mom tells me that everything changed for her one day when my three-year-old self walked over to her bed and asked her if I was a bad person. When she asked why, I said it was because she cried all the time. After that, she decided to live for me.

She got out of bed, started caring for both myself and her again, and joined a self-help group for family and friends of alcoholics.

She learned how to live on her own two feet, and even found the courage to leave my father. However, in February 2000, my dad finally sobered up, my parents slowly repaired their relationship, and they called off the divorce.

My dad has been sober ever since and at the time of writing this, he has been sober for almost 20 years. He has been sober for almost 20 years, the perfect father and husband. Mom still swears to this day that I was the gift that woke them up and taught them that life is not all about themselves. I realized much later on that I was the thing that saved my parents' marriage.

Five years after I was born, my little sister Megan came into the picture. She takes after my mother, being extremely loving and passionate. For as long as I've known her, she's been a softie for everyone.

*

When my mom was a teenager working at a local store, she met a wonderful woman who would come in often with her many children. One of her children, a little boy with a runny nose, absolutely melted my mom's heart. The boy's mother explained that he was a foster child who had been exposed to cocaine in the womb. The woman told my mom that she was going to adopt him 'because no one else could see the beauty God had created.' From the moment she met that little boy, my mom vowed to herself that she too would help God's creations.

And so came the foster children. My mom fulfilled her dream in 2006, when I was nine years old, by obtaining her foster license. Not too long after that, we received our first baby, Adam. Adam was a three-month-old boy who came to us from an eighteen-year-old mom, who had horribly abused him, both physically and mentally. I remember seeing him for the first time and being tongue-tied with shock. There were cuts and bruises on his face, from his forehead to his chin, and even his earlobes had been bruised from constant squeezing. When my mom gave him a bath not too long after he arrived, my horror was further magnified at seeing what had happened to the rest of his body.

Holding him for the first time brought out a kaleidoscope of emotions in me. It was obvious that he was very scared of everything and I didn't blame him. He had been through hell and back. I remember thinking that he was going to be afraid of us, that it was up to us to show him the good in humanity, to have a positive impact on his life.

The next six months were very hard. Adam was not easy to take care of. Because of his past living situation, he constantly acted out. He would scream and kick wherever he was, leaving no peace in the house. So Mom and Dad were always there for him, holding him, taking care of him, paying him attention. For a while, I understood that was what he needed. But then I started to feel jealous of the time they spent on him, and resentful of him too. I could see how much he stressed my parents out. And it was hard to have no quiet in the house, to be up all hours with a crying baby. I felt like I was never able to think.

I didn't have to worry for long though. Just as fast as he came, Adam left. He ended up going to his grandmother after she won custody of him.

*

It was March of 2008 and I was 11 years old. I was in class, a local Catholic school, and spent the entire day anxiously anticipating the arrival of another baby in our home. The unknown always made me nervous. I had no idea who this little baby would be or what the effect would be in my life. After Adam, I was at least fairly used to the process, but a new baby still meant there would be some kind of disruption. Whether that was good or bad was yet to be found out, and that made me very anxious.

I don't think I paid attention to anything other than my racing thoughts that day.

Before I knew it, the end of the school day was upon me. Digging through my locker looking for the correct books, I had a feeling that this day was going to change the course of my entire life. Somehow, I knew this one would be special.

And, as a matter of fact, I was correct.

I stepped out of the school gates and saw the car waiting for me there, Mom in the front seat, smiling at me. Cautiously, I walked to the car and opened the door. And I saw, for the first time, our second foster child, Aidan. Aidan was a beautiful two-week-old baby with the most gorgeous blue eyes I had ever seen. During the pregnancy, he had been exposed to cocaine, which is why they had to take him from his mother directly after he was born.

In the years since, being exposed to drugs has taken quite a toll on his life. His entire childhood, Aidan has been in and out of the hospital with various illnesses. At one point, he was eating out of a tube and had an unknown black spot on his brain. They told us that he would never walk, nor speak. Eventually, he was diagnosed with autism. For a while, we didn't think he was going to make it out of any of it. Now, he is the craziest, talkative, and happiest child I have ever known.

But I can't say it was always easy with him. Living with a child with special needs is not hard. The house was always chaotic, and I often had to take care of him, giving my parents some reprieve from his constant demands. I babysat all the time and like to think I helped raise him somewhat.

It came as no surprise to anyone when we decided to adopt him. He continued to go on monthly visits with his mother until she eventually lost all of her rights in court. The adoption process took years, but we persevered, fighting for him, and then this baby who showed up on my doorstep one day became my brother in every sense.

13

CHAPTER 2

'Andrew, what's wrong?' I hear my mom's voice, but barely.

I shake my head and try to ground myself. A million thoughts run through my head.

I am at the museum.

I am with my family.

We are supposed to be having a good time.

Stop freaking out.

My thoughts seem to have the opposite effect. My breathing speeds up and my heart flutters. There appears to be a 50-pound weight sitting on my chest. I gasp for air, trying to catch my breath.

'Andrew.' Mom's voice sounds like a distant echo.

There are too many people.

They are going to crush me.

It's so loud.

'Andrew, snap out of it.'

There are too many people.

Billions of germs around me.

Getting into my skin, contaminating my body.

I'm going to die.

I'm going to die.

I don't answer my mom. I can't. If I open my mouth, I'll die. I know it, for sure. I can smell the people and I swear I can smell the germs and I can feel my stomach turning.

I'm trapped inside my own anxiety.

*

I've always felt anxious, worrying about things, letting thoughts consume me. Even when I was a child, I'd constantly feel stuck in my own head. Since an infant, I've had trouble sleeping because I'm always worrying about anything and everything. I have memories of me constantly fiddling with my hands and tapping my foot because I had so much nervous energy, at school or at home or at the doctors. The thought *What if* ran through my head, over and over again, and I've always felt on edge, ready for something bad to happen at any time.

I like to describe anxiety as being stuck inside a haunted house 24 / 7, 365 days a year, walking around corners and trying hard not to look into windows or mirrors in case something's looking back at you. And maybe you'll get through the entire thing without a single thing jumping out, but that feeling of being nervous, of constant anxiety, is still there.

And being on edge all the time is exhausting. By the end of the day, I always feel so tired, my body worn, but then sleep is hard to come by, my thoughts keeping me up. And by the time I get to bed, it's so late that when I wake up, I feel like I've had no sleep at all.

But I got used to it. I accepted that this was the way life was for me. I wasn't even aware that there was a different way of living. I just thought being nervous all the time, filled with this energy that went nowhere, unable to sleep because of all the thoughts in my head wouldn't be quiet, was just the way everyone lived.

So I felt able to function in life the way everyone else did.

But when I was nine years old, I learned that not everyone feels the way I do. I don't remember what inspired this change in my thoughts but I began to see myself as different from everyone else. I started to go downhill. The anxiety started to change into something sinister. To this day, I'm not sure why this happened, but it felt extremely sudden.

School became harder, much harder than it had been before, and life was starting to get more complicated. Aidan was living with us full-time, which meant my home was complete chaos. I couldn't find a single place inside the house to be at peace with myself, to be still. My thoughts would loop over and over inside my head, like a broken record. And they never stopped coming. Before, a thought would appear in my mind and though I would fixate on it, it would disappear a few minutes later, like it was never there and, most of the time, it wouldn't come back, just replaced by something else. Now, however, the anxiety felt very different. The thoughts would tell me I needed to do something, and they wouldn't leave until I had completed the task. I would do that task and then a new thought would pop into my head a few minutes later, and that wouldn't leave until I did the thing it wanted me to do.

I was trapped inside my own brain.

I couldn't do anything. I couldn't do my homework, I couldn't get anywhere on time, I couldn't go out in public.

I was completely terrified of disease and germs and dirt during this time. I could see the germs crawling everywhere: the floor, the surfaces of tables, my hands. Everything was dirty. And I didn't want to get sick.

I couldn't go to restaurants with my family because I felt like there were germs just waiting for me everywhere. I couldn't stop thinking about the people who were making my food, if they had washed their hands, how they were touching everything. And what about the people who had sat in the chairs before me?

Sometimes, we'd go to places that had booths and I would have a panic attack if was forced to sit in the middle, my own personal slice of hell. I'd have to sit on the edge, because otherwise I was right in the middle of everything with no escape.

I couldn't go to the movies, because I didn't want to sit in the same chairs as people I didn't know. I hated public transport. I could barely walk outside because I knew there were germs just waiting for me.

I couldn't go anywhere.

I was convinced that it would take the smallest contamination, a brush with a hand or a handle, and that would be it for me.

My hands were raw, cracked, and bleeding from constantly washing my hands. I would wash my hands over and over again, damaging my skin until my hands were bright red.

A recurring stressor for me would take place in class. I'd be sitting there, working so hard not to touch my desk that was clearly contaminated. Inevitably, my hand would accidentally brush against the desk. *You're going to get sick. There are germs crawling all over your hand.* These thoughts would loop, over and over and over and over again. I'd try to focus in class but all I could think about was the germs crawling into my skin, heading for my heart, clogging up my lungs, my body would start to shake, my heart beating like crazy. *The germs are going to infect me, I'm going to get sick, I'm going to die.* I'd run down the hall to the bathroom, rushing to the sink, filling my hands with way too much soap, scrubbing for at least five minutes. After, I'd get a paper towel to wipe off the water and blood coming out of the many cracks in my hands. But it wasn't over then. I'd walk to the door and one more thought would rush in: *One more time. Just to be safe.* So I'd have no choice but to scrub my hands raw once again. And then a third time too. And on the way back from the bathroom, I'd realize that I washed my hands an odd amount of times, and that didn't feel right to me. So I would run back to the bathroom to wash my hands one more time.

Touch the light switch, my brain says.

No, I say. *That's stupid. There's no reason to do that.*

Just do it. You have to.

No.

If you don't do it, something bad will happen to you.

That doesn't make sense.

It does.

And then I think, *Well it wouldn't hurt to do it just in case ...*

All I have to do is walk over to the light switch and touch it. My anxiety washes away instantly. And if I don't do it, my thoughts overcome me for the rest of the day.

Giving in seems like the only solution.

Just as that thought goes away, another one pops into my mind: 'Now make sure the door is shut all the way.'

And just like that, the spiral begins again.

After a while, Mom and Dad started to notice my hand washing ritual. They'd try to tell me that I didn't need to wash my hands that many times, trying to be rational and logical, but none of us knew anything about what was going on with me, so we had no idea how to fight it. We just thought I was a germaphobe.

One of the most frustrating parts of being mentally ill is knowing that the thoughts inside my head aren't logical. But I still listen to the thoughts and am controlled by them.

With my aversion to germs came some other phobias. For one, I was completely terrified of throw up. Not that anyone *likes* throw up, but my fear was taken to the extreme. If someone even let out a small cough that sounded like it might turn into something more, I'd sprint out of the room in a flash.

One time in the fourth grade, a girl threw up in the trash can while we were playing a game. Boy, did I shut down. I wanted to be anywhere but there. I just wanted to sprint out of the school. But I couldn't. I was trapped there. I stood in the back of the room by the lockers, shaking and hyperventilating in fear. No one noticed. I was suffering alone, trapped in a hell of my own making.

As soon as I got out of that classroom, I washed my hands about six times. At lunch-time, I ate nothing, worried that I would throw up too if anything passed my lips, and that continued for about a week. I was starving myself but it felt better than the alternative.

I couldn't be on elevators either because I was convinced the ropes would break and we would fall to our deaths. That or we would get stuck forever with no one coming to our rescue. I also couldn't be around crowds: too many people meant too many germs. I remember being on class field trips to museums, feeling like I couldn't breathe because of the amount of people around me.

One day, I was at the aquarium with my family and the moment I walked in, my anxiety flared. There were so many people in the entryway, we could barely move, shoulders pressed against us, the general rumble of people so loud, I couldn't hear anything else. I couldn't breathe, From the moment we entered that museum, all I wanted to do was go into the bathroom and wash my hands, to be clean. But I couldn't find anything, so I walked along, trying to make myself as small as possible, so I wouldn't touch anyone. And then we got in, straight into the cafeteria.

It felt like the loudest place in the world. Kids screaming, laughing, talking, eating their food. I could see kids talking with their mouths full, spraying food on the tables, and I wanted to run straight out. It felt like I was stuck in a horror film.

For me, when I get anxious, my other senses become heightened. I can see things that I couldn't before, lights and colors brighter, vivid, and I can smell things that I might never have noticed before, and everything seems a hundred times louder.

So that's how I felt in the cafeteria of that aquarium. The whole world felt like it was operating in fast-forward. My family probably thought I was daydreaming, just standing there staring off into space. I may have looked pretty calm but I was definitely not. In the end, I got through the day but when I think about the day, I don't think about the things I saw, I just think about the cafeteria and those children.

And this behavior didn't go away whenever I came back home. Everything had to be perfectly lined up on every table and shelf in my room, otherwise I would feel out of control. I spent hours rearranging the objects around me, making sure they were in perfect lines. If I didn't rearrange the objects, the anxiety would gnaw at me and I wouldn't be able to stop thinking about how they were out of place.

I remember panicking because not everyone would push in their chairs perfectly in class, or not being able to focus because items were scattered all over kids' desks. I would fight the urge to put the chairs straight, to push them in properly, to order people's things. I knew that I couldn't do that to them, but to fight the urges, I would have to let the thoughts run through my head, over and over again.

I also went to the bathroom every 5–10 minutes, even if I didn't have to. I didn't only go to wash my hands, which I did all the time, but I feared that I wouldn't be able to find a bathroom when I actually needed to go. So I peed a lot, even if I didn't really have to go, forcing myself. Again, I knew these behaviors weren't logical, but I had no space for logic because these behaviors made me feel better. In this hard world where I felt like I had no control of anything around me, following these compulsions made me feel like I had control of myself, at least.

The kids at school eventually started to notice my particular fears and compulsions. And, as some kids are wont to do, they found it hilarious that the thoughts scared me so much. Groups of boys would walk by me and let out a spray of spit onto the surface of my desk. Kids would lick their hands and chase me, trying to touch me with their germy hands, and I would try my best to run away from them. They made fun of how nervous I always was, with no consideration of how I felt. I would spin into a panic attack, and they would just stand there and laugh.

As an adult, I know that they didn't know what mental illness was at that age. Hell, I didn't even know what was going on with myself. But they knew I was different and they made sure that I knew that too, no matter what.

Slowly but surely, I became that 'weird kid' at school. The one who no one wanted to hang out with except for the other 'weird' ones. I was talked about and laughed at behind my back. People avoided sitting with me at the lunch table. No one wanted me to play with them at recess.

At the time, I recognized that I was being bullied but I didn't tell anyone or try to do anything about it. I was too scared that if I told on them, it would just make matters worse and they would hate me even more. And even though I knew that they were horrible people for making me feel this way, I still wanted to be their friend, still wanted them on my side.

After a while, I started to believe the bullies, everything they said. I began to look at myself as weird, different, and separate from everyone else. Even today, I still struggle not to look at myself like that, their taunts still ringing in my ears.

CHAPTER 3

I'm insane. I'm crazy. I'm not normal.

It's what the kids told me at school, and after some time, I began to believe them.

OCD and anxiety can make you feel completely alone, even if you are surrounded by people who love you and want the best for you. I felt completely alone because it seemed like nobody understood how I felt, why I did the actions I did. Even when I didn't feel desperately alone, I still felt that I was being judged, that everyone thought I was soft and fragile and weak, that I couldn't handle the world.

I have always worried what other people think of me. For as long as I can remember, I have wanted to appear perfect, to mask all my issues, to seem put together. I don't want anyone to see who I really am because I don't want to be looked at as weird, crazy, or weak. It's only in recent years that I've learned that it's by being open and honest about my mental illness that I will be comfortable with who I am and even help others.

After a while, my parents started to recognize that my anxiety wasn't just a fear of germs, that it was something more. Though I would only find out far later, my mother herself had struggled with similar issues throughout her entire life. In her early 20s, Mom began to feel increasingly nervous, so much so that she became afraid to ever leave the house. She started to perform constant rituals, just like I was doing, and had frequent panic attacks when things didn't happen the way she needed them to. She retreated from life, overwhelmed with the anxiety she was feeling. With the help of my dad, she decided to seek help. She began to see a therapist, who would eventually diagnose her with Obsessive Compulsive Disorder and Panic Disorder. She went through a long battle but managed to conquer her fears, controlling her thoughts, and lead a better life. Although she still lives with these disorders today, she is able to effectively manage them so that she can live a happy life, where the day-to-day is easier.

But although my mom had gone through OCD and anxiety before, my symptoms presented very differently than hers, so I don't think she recognized it right away.

One day, when I was around 10 years old, my parents told me they were taking me to see a therapist. 'I'm not going,' I told them. 'I don't want to.'

I could only picture myself sitting in a dark room, some sullen man sitting in an armchair on the other side of the room, asking me, 'And how do you feel about that?' I pictured myself being part of the crazy people, this being the official stamp on who I was.

I also didn't want to be vulnerable in front of a person I didn't know. I would have to tell them stuff that no one else knew about. About all the thoughts in my head, the way they made me feel, all the things I had kept secret from everyone around me. I was still wearing my mask.

And I also knew that it was going to be tough. I didn't want to stop doing my compulsions, because they made me feel better. I knew the therapist would want me to stop and the idea of not doing them terrified me.

So I told my parents that I could handle it on my own and I wouldn't go. I thought I had won the battle.

One fall day, they walked into my room to coax me into going. They had booked the appointment and they weren't going to take no for an answer. They tried everything, and eventually I told them I would give it a try, not for myself but for them. I could tell that they were out of their minds with worry for me, and I hated that I made them feel that way. However, I made sure they knew it was only a one-time thing, that I was going to walk in, try it, and then never go back.

I remember being in the car on the way to therapy, shaking out of fear with what felt like a world of thoughts racing through my mind at a million miles per second. After 20 or so minutes, we arrived at a decently-sized psychiatric hospital to meet a person who was going to end up being extremely important in my life: Diane, my therapist, who was an expert in anxiety and OCD. In fact, she had co-founded the OCD and anxiety program at that hospital. Over the next 12 years, I would become extremely familiar with that hospital.

We walked inside and sat in a pretty big waiting room. Not wanting to contaminate myself, I sat straight up in the plastic green chair, not daring to touch the back. I looked around at the other people, praying that I wouldn't see anyone I knew. There was an old man sitting in one corner, reading a *National Geographic*. In another corner sat an angry-looking teenage girl with black eye-liner, staring down at her feet. Her mother sat beside her, anxiously tapping her foot. A family of four sat across from us, the father desperately trying to wrangle one of his toddlers.

These are my people now. The crazies.

Before I knew it, one of the doors in front of us opened and I heard the click-clack of Diane's heels that I would come to associate with therapy.

I looked up at her, this fairly normal-looking woman, who reached her hand out to all of us, introducing herself. She said she wanted to take my parents into the room first and speak to them separately.

I don't know what they spoke about in there. I guessed that she would have asked them about our home life, how my compulsions were making me behave, how they were feeling about it all. But I didn't know for sure, and a part of me didn't want to know, didn't want to hear what my parents were saying about it.

Eventually, they came back, and Diane told me that she was going to take me to do an evaluation.

I walked with Diane through those swinging gray doors to a small, dimly lit room. The second I walked in, I saw a long couch for me to lie on. I started to get nervous and wondered whether she wanted me to lie down on there and I just knew I didn't want to, that somehow that would feel like the end of everything. But Diane only asked me to take a seat. She sat herself down herself in a comfy looking armchair across from me. For a while, she didn't say anything, and I tried not to look around the room, tried to just focus on her.

After some silence, she asked me a series of questions about my life, thoughts, and the behaviors I did. When I'd heard the word evaluation, I'd thought that she was going to make me sit down and do some kind of exam, but it was actually just a simple conversation that didn't even take that long. She asked me what I worried about, and what my day-to-day schedule consisted of. She asked me how my worries interfered with my everyday life.

It was pretty scary opening myself up to a complete stranger. I knew she was a professional, that she had seen other people like me, maybe hundreds of them, but I still worried about her judging me. Even though I was there to talk about myself and my problems, I still wanted to present myself as perfect.

I also couldn't help feeling that the whole thing was an invasion of my privacy. Who was this woman that got to know all this private information about me? I felt angry about it, that she got to hear all the things that were wrong with me.

I'd spent so long wearing this mask, I could barely take it off.

But Diane was good at her job. She made me feel comfortable in myself, comfortable enough to answer her questions and open up. After a while, it didn't even feel like we were strangers anymore, like we had known each other for a while.

She understood that I was no longer living a happy life, that I was sad all the time, that my anxiety had made life unbearable.

After that initial conversation, Diane diagnosed me with Obsessive Compulsive Disorder. I'd never heard of it before but when she explained it to me, I related to it completely. It explained my excessive thoughts and compulsive behaviors, why my brain never seemed to shut up.

I felt relieved, like a great weight had been taken off my shoulders. I finally knew what was going on with me, why my brain worked the way it did. And even better, Diane told me that Obsessive Compulsive Disorder (OCD) could be controlled after some work with her.

Right then, I stopped feeling alone and like no one understood me. Diane had listened to me, understood me, saw me, and gave me hope for the future.

From that day on, OCD became a part of my identity.

Diane explained that she had openings in her schedule to take me on for 'exposure and response' therapy. This was a type of counseling where she would purposefully expose me to my biggest fears, desensitizing myself to them.

When she explained it to me, it felt like all my nightmares were going to be presented to me at once. But Diane was nice, familiar, safe, so I decided to trust her. My mother agreed to set up an appointment, and the next week, we were there.

Diane and I jumped into exposing myself to my fears right away.

First, Diane asked me to list all my fears and compulsions and rate them from what gave me most anxiety to the least. This rather large list had a fear of germs right at the top and a compulsion to tighten my shoelaces at the bottom. Looking at it like that, all in one place, felt a bit overwhelming. It seemed like so much, too much, and I wondered if I could possibly do it all. It didn't feel possible. That familiar pang went through my stomach: *This could take years. Am I going to be able to live like this for that long?*

Diane reassured me: 'Don't look at the big picture. One step at a time, and we'll get there sooner than you may think.'

We decided to start with my fear of elevators. That first week me, my mom, and Diane walked into the hospital's elevator and sat in it for just 15 minutes to start. It might not sound like much but for me, it was a huge deal. I sat on the floor, my heart racing, my palms sweaty, my lungs tight. I felt like I could barely breathe and I wanted to get out, to run away.

However, Diane just said in her calm but firm voice, 'What's the worst thing that could happen right now?'

'We could die,' I said.

'How can you challenge that thought?' she said, a phrase that I would end up hearing a lot, something I regularly say to myself now.

'This elevator is regularly checked for safety and they wouldn't let it be used if it was safe,' I quickly muttered, not fully believing it.

'Exactly right!' she said happily.

This was the first time I had ever challenged one of my OCD thoughts, and it marked a huge moment for me. For once, I had hope that I could conquer this.

Having this therapy felt like torture at times, but when I look back at it, I know that it truly saved my life. The life I was living before was no life at all, a type of torment I wouldn't wish on anyone. My thoughts controlled me and I felt like I was just surviving, jumping from one compulsion to another to make myself feel a little better.

However, if I thought living with these thoughts was hard, it was even harder resisting them. I didn't even realize just how bad I was suffering until I tried to overcome my OCD. The thoughts had become the norm for me, a part of my everyday life. Suffering was just the usual for me; I barely knew anything different. Diane taught me how to pay attention to my thoughts and recognize which ones were irrational. Then she taught me how to challenge them. Normally, I would have a thought and then do a behavior to gain relief from the thought. Now, I needed to recognize the thought was irrational and then sit with my thoughts and anxiety, not doing anything at all.

Sitting on an OCD thought without doing any compulsions is extremely uncomfortable. I would feel sick and shaky, my chest tight, my heart racing.

Go check your bedroom door to make sure it's closed all the way, my brain would say.

Nope, that has to be irrational.

Just do it.

No, who cares if it's closed all the way or not.

Something bad will happen.

How can something bad happen because my door isn't closed all the way?

However, my brain would repeat the thought over and over again: *Check the door. Check the door. Check the door.* By the time I gave in or not, it would be time for bed and I hadn't done any of my homework because I was too focused on the damn door.

This became a pretty typical scenario for me. Challenging a thought was extremely hard and wasn't just a one-time thing, I had to do it every few seconds, as the thought kept coming back into my mind. I would just have to sit it out until the thought eventually went away. And then another came in, and another, and another. It felt like I was trapped in an endless cycle. Some might have felt hopeless, but I kept going because Diane kept reassuring me that the more I did it, the easier it would get. And she wasn't wrong.

One of the biggest hurdles to jump was definitely my fear of germs. To combat it, we would sit week after week in the hospital cafeteria, Diane telling me to put my back against the booth and put both hands flat on the table. At one point, I was so scared, I could only touch the table for a second, finding myself quaking in my seat. However, I eventually got to the point where I wasn't afraid to touch the table at all, both palms resting flat on it. I was making progress.

But it wasn't that simple or easy. I began to figure out that recovery is like a roller coaster. One minute, I would resist one of my many urges and be on a high; the next, I would be back at the sink scrubbing my hands. I would fail constantly and give in to my compulsions, but for every few failures there would be a win. For a while, the wins felt like they were coming after a lifetime of failures. However, over time, they got more and more frequent. And each win would motivate me further in my recovery.

At first, when I was on the bottom of the roller coaster, I would get extremely angry at myself. I would constantly ask myself *Why am I like this?* and *Why me?* I would get so mad at myself each time I failed. I tried to focus on the wins, and at first, it was hard, because there were so few. But over time, the wins came more and more, and they made me feel good, victorious.

Another issue to overcome was my fear of throw up, and Diane's tactic for this was something I'm not going to forget easily. For months, Diane would pull up YouTube videos on her laptop of people throwing up. I would have panic attacks in that small room, only being able to look at the videos for a second before tearing my eyes away. For me, those 45 minutes were complete torture. I would sit, frozen to my chair, staring at the video screen, trying not to throw up myself. My breathing would speed up and I would be unable to think about anything other than the fact that I needed to get out of this room. However, just as it worked with the germs, eventually I started to become desensitized to the videos. Diane once again worked her magic on me.

Diane freed me from my own head. Although I knew I was always going to have OCD, I now had learned the coping skills to control it.

CHAPTER 4

Recovery is a never-ending process. I am still recovering today and will be recovering 30 years from now. There will be times in my life where my mental illness will be bad, and there will be some where it is good. I have come to accept this about myself.

My first journey to recovery from OCD was a difficult one to wage. By the end of my battle, I wasn't just some innocent kid going through life. I was a soldier who had returned home from war.

I matured fast. I had to, to get through it all.

*

The school system, as it is in America, was extremely harmful for my mental health, as it can be for many other individuals. As said by Dr. Gray, Ph.D. in *Psychology Today*, '[t]he available evidence suggests quite strongly that school is bad for children's mental health.'[1]

Every day, children wake up before eight in the morning after staying up late doing the homework that their teacher assigned to them the day before. They are forced to sit in classes they might not want to be in, learning things they have no interest in, graded in one way despite being so very different. And that's not mentioning the social pressure children are under, to achieve certain grades by their parents, to be on certain paths.

Or the fact that bullying can become rampant among children in environments like this.

I feel like the American schooling system is built to be as stressful as possible, and with stress comes mental illness.

For me, I don't think I was built for mornings. I found this out very early on. Since I was younger, waking up in the morning has always felt impossible. And to add to that, I wake up every morning expecting something to go wrong, with many various possibilities running through my head, all of them negative. It's a constant struggle.

Sleeping has always been an escape for me, as it's one of the few times I don't feel any anxiety. In a way, I self-medicate by sleeping. Whenever I'm having a dark time or fall into an anxiety spiral, I tend to retreat into sleeping all day.

And then there was the bullying too. It was starting to erode my mental health in a whole new way, even with all that Diane had thought me. For the longest time, I didn't tell my parents about it, because I felt ashamed of myself for it, but eventually I did because I just couldn't take it anymore. I wanted someone to fix it. And they were, as you might expect, not okay with it. They could see it was affecting my self-esteem and wanted to take me out of that hostile environment as soon as possible.

Every night, I would be up late into the night doing homework, crying at my desk. It felt like torture and my parents recognized that in me. Homework was causing me a ton of anxiety, and everything felt like it was going too fast for me.

The many ways the school system let us down is why, in the seventh grade at just 12 years old, my family decided to switch me and my sister from a private school to being homeschooled. My parents hadn't considered homeschooling before, but a few of our family friends did it with their children and after speaking to them, my mother was convinced that it would be the best thing for us.

So we made our excuses to our friends in school and parted with the traditional American way of schooling.

For the first time in years, I was truly happy. I was able to choose what I wanted to study, the curriculum I wanted to use, and how fast to advance in every subject. Not to mention, I was no longer seeing the individuals who used to bully me. I was able to get more sleep, finish my school in a few hours every day, and have more time to do the things I wanted to.

Homeschooling truly brightened my life in a remarkable way and made it easier to keep control of my OCD using everything Diane had taught me. It had been hard to control my thoughts and behaviors at school because not only was it hard to control that environment, I was under so much stress and anxiety from school work and bullies. Homeschooling took away much of my anxiety and freed up some space to devote to my recovery.

Although I knew homeschooling was going to be good for me, our first year, the seventh grade, was rather boring, as we were still figuring out how it worked. We bought our curriculums (there are special curriculums made for homeschoolers) and barely left the house, my mom just teaching us everything on her own. In Illinois, it's pretty relaxed when it comes to homeschool laws. There is no government oversight of grades and you do not need to submit any kinds of exams (other than the ACT, if you want to get into a college). I wanted to go to college, so we made sure to take all of the classes most colleges required. When it came time to apply to college, we would, of course, create our own transcripts.

It was just me, my mom, and my sister home during the day, which, although boring, brought us closer together.

After our first year of homeschooling, it became much more exciting. Not only did we find our feet but we learned from some friends of ours that there was a large community of fellow homeschoolers in the area. That second year, we joined a couple of what are called 'homeschool co-ops.' These are groups of homeschoolers who get together at a location to learn concurrently. As a group, the parents either teach in their area of expertise or they hire a teacher to instruct the kids.

We joined two co-ops and my mom began teaching art classes. One was at a local homeschooling family's house and the other was at a church a few towns over. They were each one day a week, one on Mondays and the other on Fridays, and both were Christian-based. After joining those, the only subject I did at home was Math, and I was a part of those co-ops until graduation from high school.

Growing up, my family practiced religion heavily. We were churchgoers every Sunday, went to Sunday school, and prayed every night before dinner and bed. However, around when I started high school, we stopped practicing it. Although my family always had a general belief in a god, we had started to question Catholicism in general. Over time, we stopped practicing, my parents becoming more 'spiritual', as they would put it.

The homeschool community in my area was very Christian heavy. Many of these people brought their religion to a level I had never seen before. As someone who was not too religious at the time, I often felt extremely judged and looked at differently for not being as religious as the rest.

The co-ops I belonged to seemed to be split right down the middle, with one side made up of those who took their religion very seriously and the other of those that didn't. Although most of my friends were from the latter group, I did make friends with some of the very heavy Christians.

*

'Okay, who wants to volunteer?'

I stand in the back of the group, feeling very queasy and shaking slightly. We are at a farm on an eighth-grade field trip, and we had just spent the last 10 minutes passing around a little hen and bonding with her. I fell in love with that little chicken the moment I saw her. I'd always loved animals and looked at them differently than most people did, seeing their humanity where most people did not. When my mom served meat at the dinner table, to me, it felt like eating another human.

My friend Tom raises his hand, steps forward, and picks up the ax. I watch the farmer stretch the chicken's neck over a log. Then Tom swings down. Everything goes black.

I close my eyes as hard as I possibly can, put my fingers in my ears. But no matter how hard I try, I still hear the thud of the ax hitting the log. I open my eyes a little too soon, only to see the chicken, without a head, run around for about 20 seconds before she flops down on the ground.

*

The day after that field trip, I stopped eating meat and dedicated my life to helping animals. Nothing was going to stop me. I made it my purpose in life.

During my five years of homeschooling, where I was able to control my OCD thanks to what Diane had taught me, I became intensely ambitious. Because of my love for animals, I became increasingly involved in the animal rights movement. By the time I was 13, I had founded my own animal advocacy nonprofit. I was on youth advisory boards for organizations such as The Humane Society of the United States, Mercy for Animals, and PETA. I did internships with organizations in high school that most people did in college. Because of my work, I won awards that some of the top people in the animal rights movement have won, all before the age of 18. I was increasingly told I would be the next leader of the animal rights movement, and boy was that a lot of pressure.

I was a teenager of strong moral principle and who did not back down in the face of oppression. At this point in my life, I was more confident in myself than I had ever been. I was ready to take on the world, and I had high hopes that I would be on to big things in my life.

But being looked at as a promising upcoming figure in the animal rights movement had its downsides. I felt like I always had to be producing something, one-upping myself, and making myself look successful all the time. It was a lot of pressure, and I felt like a loser if I wasn't constantly moving forward. I was addicted to the feeling of success, and I wanted to be the top person in my industry.

When I was 16, I won the Young Animal Rights Activist Award, which some of the most well-known animal rights activists in the movement have won. I'd strived to win this award for years. One year, I learned that I had been nominated but didn't win. I was heartbroken. And then the following year, I won, and I had never felt so good. It was like I was floating in the clouds.

But I didn't just spend those five years working. I also had a pretty good social life. Although there was a little judgement from one group to the other in my co-ops, we all got along fairly well, and I found my own group of friends who were more like me. They were solid and supporting of everything I did, and I always felt like they were looking out for me.

I also made some friends in my theater group, something I joined when quite young. It became a huge part of my life, almost as huge my activism, the type of community that I still haven't been able to replicate. It truly felt like we were a family, and that's how I've always looked at them.

During this time, I also held my first job starting in my second year of high school. When I was 15 years old, I started volunteering, doing animal care at a local nature center. I volunteered one day a week, then two, then three, until I was working full-time.

I was extremely ambitious and soon knew how to do everything the staff members did. I became increasingly close to my boss, Pam, and a year later, the week of my 16th birthday, she offered me a job. For the next four years, I worked at this nature center, and I was so proud of not only having it but the kind of work I was doing.

At this job, I met two of my best friends, still some of the most important people in my life today, Brianna and Amylynn, otherwise called my 'sibs.' I met Amylynn first, as she was my supervisor as a volunteer. When I met her, I was just a 15-year-old with 'Justin Bieber hair' and braces. She definitely met me at one of the most awkward times of my life. Although she was older than me, we bonded fast and became increasingly close. I would increasingly confide in her about my life during work hours and she would give me advice on all things. Hence why I thought of her as the big sister I never had. It wasn't long before we were spending time together outside of work.

Brianna, meanwhile, started working with us about a year later. Although at first, I was upset she could come in between me and Amylynn, she and I also clicked right away. In fact, the three of us became very close. At work, I don't think it's an understatement to say we had the best of times together. The three of us felt like we were allowed to be our true selves with one another.

Looking back now, I'd have to say that my teenage years were some of the best in my life. Learning how to control my OCD, with a tight group of friends from my co-ops, the theater, and work, meant that I was able to let myself be myself completely. I felt loved, supported, and valued in every aspect of my life.

I thought it was all up from there. Where else was there to go?

PART TWO

COMING OUT

CHAPTER 1

I had my first crush on a guy in the sixth grade.

He was an eighth grader, which made him like a god in my mind. The eighth graders were all tall, powerful, and intimidating. One glance from them made me shake. At school, there was an unspoken rule that we didn't talk to the eighth graders, they talked to us, and if they did, we were the luckiest people in the school that day.

His name was Chris, and he sat behind me in band. He played the sousaphone. The very definition of the perfect boy for 12-year-old me.

I caught myself constantly looking behind me to steal glances at him, which, now that I look back on it all, probably made him think that I was a complete creep. Surprisingly, I wasn't the slickest kid out there.

Chris had long, flowing brown hair and was extremely tall. He had a large chin and a sharp jawline. He was extremely popular, just as all the jocks in my school were, which just made him even more powerful. Whenever I passed him in the halls, he was leaning on the lockers talking to all the coolest kids in the school. I constantly heard his name in the whisperings of the girls on the blacktop at recess and when Chris would walk by, they would just giggle.

Secretly, I longed to join that group of girls to discuss my infatuation of Chris.

I thought about Chris constantly. He was always in the back of my mind, leaving me unable to focus. When I passed him in the halls, I got this warm and fuzzy feeling in the pit of my stomach. I would dream of talking to him, of reaching out to him and introducing myself, and he would already know who I was, and, and, and … Talking to him was completely out of the picture, obviously, because he clearly didn't know I existed, and definitely wouldn't care about me if he did.

Though now I knew that I had a crush, at the time, it took me a long time to realize what was going on with me. Liking boys in a romantic way didn't even occur to me as something that I might be able to do. I'd grown up with heteronormativity inked into my brain. I knew about gay people, but I never thought I was one of them. Not until Chris.

It took one day in band, my thoughts making their usual trail towards Chris, where it just hit me out of the blue. *This is a crush. I have feelings for this boy, romantic ones.*

I clutched my saxophone tightly and began to panic. Ironically, the more panicked I got about what I was feeling, the more I started to think about him in romantic ways. In my house, in my room, even walking down the aisle towards me, dressed in a wedding suit. *No, this isn't natural. What am I doing? What does this mean?*

I rushed home from school, slammed my bedroom door shut, and waited for my dad to return from work. I had to find out what was going on with me and I was certain that my dad would have all the answers. I sat on my bed contemplating all of the explanations. *There's something wrong with me. Or maybe I just really want to be his friend. Maybe I just want to be around him because he's so cool. Maybe I just really want to be around him and … NOPE.*

I quickly shoved the thoughts into the deepest parts of my brain. There was no way I was gay. No way.

A little after five in the afternoon, I heard the back door open, the jingle of my dad's keys ringing in my ears. I stayed there, frozen on my bed, wondering what my dad would think when I asked him about this crush. *Is he going to think I'm weird, wrong, perverted? Is he going to be disappointed in me? Is he going to be sad?*

For what felt like hours, I had an internal battle in my head about whether telling him was a good idea or not. Eventually, one side won out and I inched my way off the bed and towards his room. I couldn't struggle with this alone anymore. I needed answers.

The door was open and I shuffled my way in. Before I had time to change my mind, I just blurted it out:

'Dad … is it normal to have a crush on a boy?' I asked, a nervous tremor finding its way into my voice.

He looked at me for a second, surprised, and I could see him trying to puzzle together an acceptable answer in his brain.

'Yes, every boy goes through a phase like that. It'll pass, don't worry about it.'

And he had nothing else to say about it. Hearing that made me feel better, the fear that I was wrong gone.

So I shoved my feelings for this boy deep down inside of me and pretended like they didn't exist. I convinced myself that this attraction to men was just a phase and would soon pass. I pointed my attention towards girls and tried my absolute best to have crushes on them. And it worked … or at least, seemed to.

I had my first relationship with a girl the summer before eighth grade, a year after I'd started to homeschool, with Audrey, who I'd met through my theater group and was also homeschooled. We had the classic 13-year-old relationship, where we just called each other boyfriend and girlfriend and did nothing but hold hands. But I didn't mind that it went nowhere else. I had a girlfriend and that was all that mattered.

During that three-month relationship, I remember having such an amazing time. We had a regular group of friends that we hung out with every weekend, and we would spend hours in one of our friend's basement, mini-golfing, and playing games in the local park. It was a middle schooler's dream summer.

However, towards the end of the summer, Audrey broke up with me, telling me that I was too needy. I don't know if she was lying to cover up the fact that she didn't have romantic feelings for me (or that possibly there was someone else she wanted to pursue), but I don't remember being needy at that time. I was sad after we broke up, but it didn't take me too long to get over it. After, we ended up staying close friends for a long time.

I had a second girlfriend later on in the eighth grade, with a girl I had originally met through my Catholic school. During that relationship, I remember how our friends would urge us to kiss, how I would try to work up the nerve to do it. One part of me really wanted to; another part of me really didn't. I felt like there were expectations placed on me to perform in a certain way, to do what was expected of a typical straight boy of that age.

Even with everything that Diane had taught me, I was still really anxious about how I presented myself to people, wondering if I was living up to what a 'normal' guy should be. I watched my friends in relationships, trying to be like them, but not truly putting any heart into it. Being in the eighth grade, my guy friends were just starting to become interested in girls physically. They began to talk about girl's bodies and one time, a friend asked me if I'd got to touch her boobs yet. I remember being surprised that he'd asked me that and then embarrassed because I had never thought about doing that before, and then I started wondering why I'd never thought about it, if I should have thought about it, what it meant that I hadn't.

'Not yet, but boy do I want to,' I said, lying.

I never did kiss her before the breakup, much to my friends' dismay. But, let's be honest, I wasn't too upset about it. And I certainly never touched her boobs.

With my sophomore year of high school came my third and last girlfriend (thank goodness for that). It was still a rather innocent relationship, for clear reasons. Throughout this relationship, we frequently double-dated with another couple, which led to me copying what they were doing in order to have a 'real relationship'. They held hands so we held hands. They cuddled so we cuddled. He kissed her so ... I missed and got her nose.

I loved double-dating with that other couple, mostly because I had the biggest crush on the other boy. I never acknowledged it to myself, not out loud, not even inside my head, but I knew it to be true. I found him so attractive, and I remember thinking he smelled like heaven. I'd lean on every single word that he said. Double-dating meant I got to spend time with him and picture myself in his girlfriends' place, all while holding my own girlfriend's hand. The perfect situation for your local closeted gay boy.

Looking back now, I find most of this to be little funny anecdotes about my time pretending to be straight. But, at the time, being in denial of who I was took me through a great deal of sadness. I tried so desperately to be like the other boys, the 'normal' ones, and I constantly felt like I was failing. Sometimes, I would feel intense hatred and anger towards myself because I wasn't perfect, because I was different, because I was 'wrong'. And then I would feel the thickest sadness, so much of it that I could barely breathe, and I wanted nothing more than to be free, but I didn't even know how I'd become imprisoned.

CHAPTER 2

I have never truly felt part of anything.

Even when I'm in a group of friends, I've always felt like I was both in the group and outside of it, somehow both staring in and looking out. I love my friends, so much, but I often feel these feelings at the same time. Even with the friends I am closest to, I've always felt a sense of separation from them, a distinct feeling that I am just inherently different from them in some way. I have never felt like I belong.

I find myself constantly thinking that everyone secretly hates me, that they talk about me behind my back all the time. I find myself wondering what they're judging me on, any glance somehow filled with meaning, every look over a shoulder.

These thoughts are not logical, but they persist.

So pretending to be straight inside all of this was terrifying. I was already convinced people were talking about me constantly. Hiding a whole part of myself on a daily basis made it even worse.

And I knew that being gay meant being different. I knew that no matter what my friends or my family thought about it, no matter how accepting or supportive they were, I would go around my entire life being different. It meant an entire lifetime of being judged by others. It meant that the dream of being perfect, of fitting in, of being 'normal', was dead.

As you might imagine, I spent a lot of my time worried that I was going to be found out, that my massive secret was going to be exposed, that I'd be outed.

When I was in the closet, I constantly felt like everyone talked about it behind my back. The sad truth is, they probably did. Talking to people who have known me since I was a kid, I've now learned that they all had some kind of idea that I was gay. They all guessed it at some point or another but didn't say anything. It seemed to be an unspoken truth on both sides of the table. In fact, there were some people who I came out to and all they said was, 'I know.' At the time, that response was a little frustrating. After all, I had tried so hard not to act 'gay' or flamboyant or camp. And now I knew that all that work was for nothing. In actuality, all the trying to not seem gay probably meant that I made it very obvious that I was.

However, at the time of my third and final attempt to be straight, I was far from acknowledging it to myself. The word 'gay' was a label that I refused to attach to myself. I didn't want to be that, couldn't be that. But, as I went through puberty, I found myself drawn more and more to these urges, and looking at cute boys wasn't enough. So I turned to the internet to satiate myself, in the darkness of my room, the door locked. My behavior surrounding this became quite self-destructive. I would race home sometimes, run into my room, reach for my laptop, and be done within a few minutes. And then after, I would feel a burning shame and guilt and I would hate myself. The next day, it would happen again.

It was during one of these times that acceptance came to me. A singular thought rolled across my mind: 'I'm gay. I really am.'

And that was it.

I went over and over the thought in my head, testing out the label, trying to see if it fit. The truth was, it had fit for years. I had just been scared about letting myself accept that.

I suddenly felt dizzy and lightheaded. All of a sudden, a wave of nausea swept through my stomach and my throat tightened. I became extremely aware of how wet my forehead was becoming and my entire body was shaking. I was paralyzed in my chair.

I knew that I had to talk to someone about this. There was no way I couldn't handle it alone.

So I told my mom I was gay the day I finally accepted it myself.

To me, my mom has always been the person I trust the most in this world and the only one that I don't feel judged by. There was no question that she was the first one I'd tell.

I remember trying to build up the courage to step out of my room and tell her. Slowly, I eased my way out of my room to her.

'Mom ... I need to tell you something...'

'What is it?' she asked.

'It's ... I'm ... The thing is ...' For some reason I couldn't get the words out of my mouth. Saying the words 'I'm gay' is the hardest thing in the world when first coming out of the closet.

'Andrew, you're scaring me,' Mom said, and I could see the fear in her eyes, hear it in her voice, and it was like we were right back there, with my OCD. 'Just say it.'

'I'm gay.'

The words felt almost like gibberish coming out my mouth.

I didn't get to see her reaction to it immediately because I was looking down at my feet, like I had done something terrible and needed to confess to her. After a few moments of silence, which felt like they had been stretched into eternity, I looked up and saw her eyes filled with tears. But I knew, instinctively, that these weren't tears of sadness.

'That's it?' she asked. 'The way you were acting, I thought you were about to tell me something horrible. You know I love you no matter what.'

I immediately started sobbing and ran into her arms. This weight, this constant stress and worry, had finally been lifted from my body. I felt a million pounds lighter.

I asked my mom to tell my dad, because I couldn't get through another conversation like this. I also decided I wasn't going to tell anyone else. For one thing, I was still very involved in the homeschool community, and as said before, they are extremely Evangelical Christian. I was sure that if they found that I would be thrown out. My theater group was also Christian-based, and I had no idea how everyone there would react. Although theater is often associated with homosexuality, I didn't know anyone in my theater group who was openly gay at the time. For right now, I had to stay partly in the closet.

CHAPTER 3

If you think being completely closeted is bad, having one foot in the closet and the other out might be even worse. Only telling my family, I had a sense of freedom and a brief relief from the anxiety of keeping my sexual orientation hidden. My dad ended up accepting me for it, even though he had told me it was just a phase to begin with.

I remember seeing him for the first time after my mother told him, and I just knew that he knew, could see it in his face, but I was too afraid to say anything. We were in the car, the kind silence that you could cut with a knife hanging around us. Finally, I just blurted it out: 'So ... you know?'

He took a second to respond. 'Yes, and you know I love you no matter what, right?'

I don't know if my dad ever meant them to be, but those words were so important to me, and they still are to this day. They remind me of how loved I am, how supported.

Eventually, I would go on to also tell my sister, who was 11 years old at the time. She was pretty young and I had no idea how she was going to react. I didn't even think she'd understand it, not entirely. I told her with my parents with me, and, to my relief, she accepted me without question. In her eyes, I hadn't changed one bit. I was still the older brother she'd had for all these years and would continue to be so. That night, she knocked on my door and told me that she had a surprise for me. Telling me to close my eyes and hold out my hands, she put something extremely light in my palms. Opening my eyes, I saw that she had drawn me a rainbow pride flag on a piece of printer paper. I don't think I've ever told her this but that small gesture of acceptance meant so much to me. Whenever my confidence goes down, I look at that pride flag that is still taped on my bedroom wall.

My brother Aidan, since my coming out, has grown up exactly how every kid should: as if homosexuality is completely normal. His entire life, we have told him that some boys marry girls and some boys marry other boys. We make sure that he knows that both types of love are the exact same thing. Now I'm able to bring a boy I'm seeing home and it's not weird or strange or out of the norm.

At the time of my accepting myself as being gay, I had a solid group of friends, most of which I knew wouldn't treat me any differently once I came out to them.

I had my group from my theater company as a teenager, which was a group of very different people, all of whom I got along with. However, two of them stood out from the rest. Audrey, who we know from earlier, was one of my closest friends. The other was a girl called Charlotte. Charlotte is pretty special to me, as we've had a friendship spanning around 11 years. We might have grown apart at certain times in or lives but we always come back together.

I told Audrey first. I sent her a text, telling her that I had something to tell her, and then just came out with it. I remember waiting for her to get back to me, waiting and waiting, and thinking I was stupid to have done it over text, that in person might have been better, but I was terrified of that. So text it was. When she replied, finally, she told me that accepted me for who I was, that she was still going to be my friend, and wanted nothing but the best for me.

And then I told everyone else, slowly but surely. I spent a lot of this time being on edge about it, nervous about telling people, scared that they weren't going to accept me. But I found that everyone was pretty supportive about it, that they accepted me for who I was, that they still loved me in the way they had before.

But even as I told people, I kept one of my friends in the dark.

Her name was Emma, and I'd met her in the fifth grade, when I was still in traditional schooling. We went to the same school and church, and her family was also in my theater group, so we were connected in multiple ways. And if that wasn't enough, her parents became friends with my parents. Before long, we started seeing them constantly. Our family, theirs, and another would meet up all the time for dinner and go on frequent outings together. Eventually, we got so close to Emma's family that we considered them to be family of our own. Emma was practically my sister.

However, Emma's family were a very conservative Catholic family and always had been, even as my family began leaning away from religion altogether. When I realized and accepted the fact that I was gay, I thought about them. I knew they wouldn't accept me. Even though I loved them so much, had spent so much time with them, I knew that there was no space for me the way I was in their lives. Part of me had hope that maybe, because I was so close to them, because I had spent so long in their lives, they might accept me. But that hope was futile. I just knew, deep down, that they wouldn't.

So, as I began to open up to other friends about my sexuality, I kept them in the dark. I just couldn't bring myself to lose them. So I stayed partially in the closet for Emma and her family. Every time I was around them, I felt on edge, scared that they might see it in me and just ask, and then I would have to tell them the truth, and they would cast me out forever.

CHAPTER 4

I met Daniel for the first time after a performance with the theater group when I was 16. He was friends with another friend of mine and had come to see her in the show. I was attracted to him the moment I saw him.

'Andrew!' my friend said, 'I want to introduce you to Daniel.' My cheeks turned red and I slunk over to them, slightly shaking. I reached my sweaty hand over and awkwardly shook his hand.

'Hi,' I said. And with that one word started the beginning of my life dating authentically.

We exchanged numbers at the show and I don't think we stopped texting for weeks. We texted all day every day, talking about anything and everything.

One day I got this text: *Hey, so I know we've been talking for a while, and I really like you, and I'd really like it if we can meet again in person. How does Saturday at Panera sound?*

My heart froze. Even though I knew I was attracted to him, I never thought he might reciprocate that. It felt surreal to me. Like it had almost just not happened.

*

From the moment Daniel sent me that text, I couldn't stop thinking about it. I was so nervous. This was my first time going on a date with a person I actually had real and authentic feelings for.

And I really wanted it to go well. I desperately wanted someone to be able to share my life with, and I really liked him.

So on that Saturday, I stood in front of Panera waiting for Daniel to arrive. Having so much anxiety about it, I'd arrived a half hour early. Those 30 minutes of just waiting around felt like an eternity, but he eventually arrived, my heart leaping as I watched him make his way over to me. We awkwardly hugged, not exactly knowing how to touch each other, ordered some smoothies, and went over to sit at a small table.

Before arriving, I'd wondered if talking to him in person would be difficult. After all, with texting him, there was time for me to think of the perfect response, no awkward waiting for someone to fill the silence. It was easy, the conversation flowing. But I had no reason to worry. Talking to him in person was no different than over text, and we talked nonstop for two hours.

One date turned into two, into three, into four. One day, while we were driving, I suddenly burst out: 'So ... what are we?'

'Oh,' he said, and he sounded a little confused. 'I kind of thought we were boyfriends.' He paused. 'Do you want to be?'

'Yes!' I said, and then, embarrassed at being so excited, 'I mean, yes. Boyfriends.'

That day, we became official and it marked a huge cornerstone in my life. I became addicted to the feeling of being myself around Daniel. I wanted to talk to and be with him 24 / 7 because the only time I felt completely free was when I was with him. Being around him felt almost like I was living a different life, one where nothing really mattered, where everything was good and better and perfect.

Most of the time, we didn't even leave his house. We would just lay in his bed, watching Netflix, usually *The Walking Dead* or some other show. We could sit there for hours, talking to one another about what felt like everything, and even though we saw each other all the time, I always left missing him.

One day, right as I was about to leave, Daniel put his arms around my waist, looked me in the eyes, and then pressed his lips softly against mine. My chest exploded. I closed my eyes and all those times I had spent watching the guy get the girl, where I had put myself into the girl's position, where I had dreamed that might happen to me at some point, were erased. I didn't need to imagine myself in someone else's love story. I was in my own.

The first thing I wanted to do after was to tell Emma. I was almost bursting with it and nearly called her the second I was out of Daniel's house. But I knew I couldn't. I was still hiding all that I was from her, which meant hiding Daniel too.

Daniel and I spent the next few dates of ours just making out. One day, while we were at his house, I felt an impulse race through me. 'That's it,' I said. 'No more hiding. I don't care what people think of me. I'm going to show you off to everyone. Let's make this Facebook-official.'

'Are you sure?' he asked. 'What about your best friend Emma and her family?'

I had told Daniel about Emma the second I thought it was good to. I had to tell him about this very important person in my life and how she and her family were, so that he understood why I didn't want to be so loud about us. But right then, I didn't think about her. I didn't think about the consequences, if any, about putting this on Facebook. I just knew that I wanted to be with Daniel.

'She doesn't have a Facebook,' I quickly said. 'It's okay. Let's do it.'

And with one press of a button, it was done.

A few days passed. I saw Emma a few times and everything seemed normal. We were even planning a trip to Wisconsin together for the following week. Any panic I had about her finding out disappeared by how usual everything seemed.

And then the text came: *Are you gay?*

I was at home and I felt almost dizzy when I looked at the text. I read it a hundred times, pouring over those three words again and again, like maybe if I kept reading them, they might change. I felt like lying to her, like telling her that no, I wasn't gay. But even thinking about saying those words felt like I was throwing myself back into the closet. I couldn't lie to her. I couldn't do that to myself.

Me: *Yes, I'm gay.*

Emma: *How could you lie to me?*

Me: *I didn't lie to you. I wasn't ready to tell you yet. I didn't know how you would feel about it.*

Emma: *This changes everything.*

Me: *No, it doesn't. I'm still your same 'brother' Andrew. I'm still the same Andrew who loves you and is always there for you.*

Emma: *Andrew, you are straying down a dangerous path that I cannot follow with you. The devil is inside of you.*

Me: *Please! This doesn't change anything!*

Emma: *Yes it does. Contact me if you want to talk about the Bible, but me nor my family can't have contact with you anymore. I will always care about you. Goodbye.*

I sat on my bed for what felt like hours, staring at that last word. *Goodbye.* I didn't know what to say back to her. I didn't know if there was anything to say. I sobbed, struggling to breathe. This was the friend I cared about most in the world, someone who had been like a sister to me, and here she was abandoning me for how I love. I didn't understand how she could do this to me.

*

Around the time Emma left me, my friends started going to college and I lost my core friend group. Due to changing circumstances in our lives, we had simply drifted apart. Not too long after that, after a passionate three-month relationship, Daniel broke up with me too. He sent me a text one day telling me that we needed to meet up and talk, that it wouldn't take too long. I knew what was going to happen the moment I read that text. And maybe if this had happened before Emma, I might have cared more about it. But I felt detached from everything. All I could think about was losing this good friend of mine, about getting her back.

I needed Emma. I had needed her my entire life without realizing it.

The day after getting that text, Daniel and I sat in a McDonalds in silence, eating our food without saying much. I thought he would do it in the restaurant but we managed to get through without anything. On the ride home, I wondered if I had overthought everything, that maybe he wasn't going to break up with me. But just as he was about to step out of the car, he turned to me: 'Andrew, I'm sorry, but I don't think we're right for each other.'

I felt like the entire world had fallen out from under me. 'Okay,' I said. I had no other words, nothing else to give.

'I'm sorry. I will always care about you. Goodbye.'

The words rang in my ears, painfully similar to Emma. He took my hand in his, smiled, and then left the car.

And for the first time ever, I felt truly, truly alone.

PART THREE

CHAPTER 1

Something inside me changed forever the day that Emma left me.

Though I'd had problems in the past, I'd always felt like I had people to lean on, supported, loved. But when Emma left me, I felt completely alone for the very first time. Sure, I had some really good friends, like Amylynn and Brianna, and I still enjoyed hanging out with them, but there was an emptiness inside me, this hollow feeling of having lost someone very important to me.

And so began something that has stayed with me all this time: a constant feeling of loneliness. Even when I'm with my family or my friends, I still feel completely empty, like I have nothing to live for anymore. I need to constantly be surrounded by people to feel something and whenever I leave, or whenever they leave, there's always a part of me that wonders if they're ever going to come back.

I also started to seriously fall into self-hatred during this time. Something that I've had to continually work to fight off since. I began to hate every single thing about myself. And, more than that, I thought that being gay was disgusting, horrible, that it was the single worst thing about me. I thought that there couldn't be anything about me that people could love. I was a waste of life.

I hated feeling this way about myself and I knew, I just knew, that if I found someone else to replace Emma, if I found someone else to fill the hole inside me, I would feel better.

So I went out to make a new friend, a replacement, as soon as possible. I went to every party I was invited to, every hangout, said yes to anything and everything. I felt like I was a hunter, searching for my prey, becoming more and more desperate with each passing day.

One day, I went to the mall with a few friends. These were new friends, found through some other friends of mine, and I didn't really know them that well. But new friends meant new opportunities to meet people. Immediately, I spotted Nick, someone I had known for a while, but only at a distance. We'd both grown up in the same theater group but hadn't spent a long time together. That day, I started to talk to him again, made plans to catch up, and we started hanging out regularly.

Slowly but surely, Nick became my person. I felt less empty and alone when I was around him. I began to crave his attention, validating myself from the way that he talked to me, what he said about me. I wanted to spend every single moment with him, becoming intensely bitter and jealous when he spent time with other people. I didn't want anyone else around him, didn't want anyone to take him away from me.

Not too long after I became close with Nick, he started dating Grace. At first, I saw her as a threat to me and Nick. I knew that he would begin to spend more time with her than he did with me and I hated that. But, after meeting her a few times, I started to become attached to her too. It felt like I had just gained another person, someone else to make me feel whole.

Nick and Grace dated a whole six months. As it turns out, neither had the highest of self-esteems either at the time. Nick increasingly struggled with depression and dark thoughts which could only be fixed when Grace was around. Grace was only happy with herself when she was around me and Nick. I felt like I needed both of them to be happy. Plus, Nick and Grace couldn't drive yet and I could, so the only way they were able to see each other was through me. So started three very unhealthy and dependent relationships.

Because I desperately wanted them to continue to love me, I would do anything for them. And when I say *anything*, I mean anything. I picked Nick up from school when he didn't have a ride home, took him anywhere he wanted to go. I paid for everything of theirs, from food when we went out to small things that they wanted. I always came with them on their dates, driving them to and from.

When I look back at it all, I now know that they were using me, that their friendship with me was wholly dependent on what I did for them. They knew that I would do anything for them, and they took advantage of that as much as they possibly could. I sometimes wish that I had seen it at the time. But thinking about how I was back then, I don't think that it would have made much difference. If anything, it would have made me feel wanted, needed, by someone. And that was everything that I wanted.

We began to become more and more dependent on each other, which led to a lot of fighting. We'd increasingly have arguments about who was spending more time with who. We began to nitpick every little thing in our friendships, causing fights between us. And then there were the arguments that they got into, which I was always trapped right in the middle of. They'd force me to choose a side and when I didn't, they'd become angry about it.

Around the end of their relationship, I began to develop romantic feelings for Nick. Maybe this was inevitable, given how much time we spent together, but it wasn't the best thing for either of us at the time. I became even more dependent on him. I literally idolized him and felt like I was deeply in love with him.

After those six months, Nick and Grace's relationship deteriorated. And because we were so intertwined, their breakup was like an implosion. Without Grace in his life, Nick became depressed and suicidal. At one point, he even told me he was going to end his life. I had to call his mom and tell her to run up to the bathroom and stop him. I saved Nick's life that night.

And then there was the picking of sides. Because I felt like I was in love with Nick, when he forbade me from seeing Grace, I just obeyed him. I cut Grace off without feeling a single thing about it.

CHAPTER 2

For as long as I can remember, I have wanted to be a veterinarian. It's all I ever dreamed of.

So when I turned 18 and it was time to attend college, it was only natural that I picked to study pre-veterinary studies. I felt so ready to jump into those four years of college at the University of Illinois in Chicago.

But when it came to the idea of living at college, I couldn't do it. Even just thinking about having so much space between me and my friends gave me intense anxiety.

Given that, I decided to commute. Looking back at it now, living at home for other people was probably not the best decision I could have made. The commute itself consisted of me driving to the train station, parking, and taking the train into my school. And then repeating that on the way back. The whole thing took out a huge chunk of my time.

Now I'm a suburban boy through and through, so I had never ever taken public transportation before. I was used to driving in a car to get to anywhere I needed to go. At first, it was exciting, this new way of traveling, but after the novelty of that wore off, I started to hate the commute entirely. First off, the train was not the cleanest place. In fact, it's pretty disgusting. I'd find things from old sandwiches on the seats to spilled smoothies and syringes on the floor. Along with that, there was also a pretty wide variety of people. Homeless people would walk down the aisles asking for any money from anyone. There were people rolling blunts on the train right out in the open. There were other offenders, drunk people trying to get a rise out of us, people who treated the train as their beds, others who chose to wear little clothes. Very quickly, my germophobic tendencies started to come up again. I became increasingly afraid of the train and, because of that, afraid of the commute, and because of that, afraid to attend school.

When I was on the train, all I could think about were the germs of the hundreds of people who passed through on the train before me. I was afraid to sit in the seats but had to force myself to. I could feel the germs crawling all over me, like I was covered in spiders, and I would sit there stiff in my seat, afraid to touch the back, all those things from my childhood coming back to me.

It was the worst when the train was super crowded. During rush hour, hundreds of commuters would cram themselves onto the train, leaving no space at all. If I got a seat, I was lucky, and even then someone would be sitting or standing very close to me. If I didn't get a seat, I would need stand, in which case someone was always so close to me that we were touching. Not to mention, I would have to touch the metal pole so I didn't fall over whenever the train slowed down or sped up. For someone with OCD, it was like hell. I sat or stood there paralyzed, desperately wishing to get off the train, trying not to think about everything around me. The moment I got off, whether I was late to class or not, I would rush to the bathroom to wash my hands five times. All I wanted to do after the commute home was take the hottest shower, burn the germs off me.

The city itself also brings up my OCD urges. I'd be at school and be afraid to touch anything, constantly washing my hands. I also dislike the city because of all the people in it. Cities mean lots of people, which doesn't exactly make the cleanest environment. From the smoky air to the sticky concrete, I felt trapped in a world of infestation.

Because of the train and the city, I avoided school completely. I would skip class after class, burrowing into my bed instead. My bed has always been a safe spot for me, away from all the stress and anxieties of the world. Most of my life, whenever I feel depressed or anxious, I've always just retreated to my bed. Sometimes I lie in my bed, zone out, and just stare at the ceiling for hours. Skipping class to spend time in my bed happened more and more frequently as the year went on.

But it didn't just stop there. With the lying in bed came the constant guilt. After all, I was paying thousands of dollars for these classes, and it was something I had wanted to do ever since I could remember. I even felt like I was letting my parents down. All of this made me feel like one of the worst humans on the planet. I wanted desperately to do well but I just couldn't get out of bed.

Because of my anxiety during my time in this life, I lost control and new OCD habits started to emerge that I'd never had before. I was quickly losing control of my life, so, of course, I had to gain control in some way. My mom would become frustrated because she couldn't open the lids of any of the jars because I would tighten them too much. I would go back to those jars and tighten them over and over again, terrified that they might be loose, to the point where my hand and wrist was in a lot of pain. I didn't care about the pain or that I might be damaging my body, all I knew was that tightening the jars made me feel better. I would constantly check to make sure that the door was locked, or the faucet was turned off all the way. I think I broke every faucet in the house that year, as I was pushing them back so tightly to make sure they were turned off. I began counting, something that I'd never done before. I had to do everything a certain amount of times, until it felt 'just right.' Although not widely known, counting is a very common symptom of OCD. People who suffer with OCD often have 'good' and 'bad' numbers. I would have to touch something a certain amount of times until it felt 'just right.'

Other times, I would count my steps and have to take a certain amount of steps to get somewhere. Sometimes, I would have to enter a room a certain amount of times or re-read a passage in a textbook until it felt right.

Counting is a very time-consuming compulsion and really took up a large chunk of my day. Over time, it began to be a huge problem because it interfered with my daily life. I was late to everything because I was counting something. I couldn't do my homework because I had to read each sentence over and over again. I knew it wasn't rational or logical, but I couldn't stop because it made me feel better. If I didn't count, the urge and thought would never leave my mind. It was only by counting that I felt better.

Along with counting, I began confessing things. I think confessing is one of the worst OCD symptoms to have. When I start down the trail of confessing, it never stops. I constantly analyze every single thing I've ever done, and always find something 'bad' I've done. I then feel like I need to tell my parents or a close friend for reassurance that I'm not a bad person. I confess something but it's never over. I then think of something else I need to confess to them. And then another, and another, and another. And until I confess what's on my mind, I can't think of anything else because I'm so overwhelmed with guilt and anxiety.

Once again, I had lost control.

I felt like I was right back where I started, like I hadn't learned a single thing. I felt like a complete failure. After such a good couple of years, I never thought I would be back in a place like this. It felt like I was stepping backwards instead of forwards. At the time, I thought that once I recovered, I would be okay forever. It wasn't until years later that I learned that recovery is never linear.

During this time, I was also constantly fixated on Nick. I felt less anxious when I was around him. We spent a lot of time together, and when I was with him, I felt alive and seen. He made me feel important. He made me feel happy about who I was. When I was with him, it was the only time in my life that I felt in control. However, my dependence on him was really taking a toll on my life. When I was in class, whenever I actually went, I couldn't focus because I would be too worried about what Nick was doing or be too preoccupied with a fight we were currently having. Just like before, we were constantly fighting. I would constantly notice every small thing he did, and anything he did that I didn't like, I would make sure that he knew about it. Sometimes, he didn't answer my texts for a couple of hours and I would explode saying he hated me. He might hang out with another friend and I would freak out, telling him he likes them more than me. I was begging him to validate me, to make me feel good about myself.

And I was so attracted to him. The moment I saw him or saw his name pop up on my phone, I would get butterflies in my stomach. He would often say nice things to me, and in the back of my head, I knew that they were platonic, but the other part of my brain convinced me he had feelings for me. Sometimes he would touch my shoulder and I would misinterpret that as flirting. It all gave me hope that maybe, somehow, some kind of way, he might just like me back.

My job at the nature center also started to take a hit because of my mental illness. When I did show up, I was late. Sometimes, I even called in and asked for someone else to cover my shift. I felt like I was destroying and sabotaging everything, even the things that I loved the most. Although I was aware of what I was doing, no matter how badly I wanted to stop, I just couldn't seem to control myself. I had a constant nervous feeling that I would soon lose everything I loved.

Somehow, I chose to take more on during my freshman year, applying for a second job. Clearly I was over committing and taking on more than I could chew. I was thrilled, as I had landed a job as a veterinary assistant at a vet clinic. Finally, I would be gaining experience towards my future and dream career. I had never been happier about a job before. At first, everything seemed to be going great and it even felt like maybe my life was righting itself. I would put on my scrubs every morning and arrive with a smile. But after a while, my thoughts started to get to me again.

I would always show up to work but it was hard for me to get out of bed and face the world most days. Waking up meant feeling large rushes of anxiety all day. So I was late every day.

Naturally, my parents became increasingly frustrated with me, because I was giving my social life more attention than my school. We kept arguing about where I was putting my focus. I wasn't getting great grades and they knew I was extremely fixated on Nick. I can imagine it was hard for them to watch me do this, to basically throw my life away for another person.

One day, my parents knocked on my bedroom door and let me know that they had made an appointment with a psychologist on my behalf, as it was obvious to them that more was going on than could be seen on the outside. I agreed to go. No fighting, no shouting, no arguing. I wanted relief.

It didn't take long before I was sat in the doctor's small office on a red leather couch, speaking about what had been happening with me. 'I can't focus in class. I'm late to everything. I'm terribly disorganized. It seems like I don't have anything together. It's really affecting my grades and jobs.'

After some follow up questions and talking to my parents, she then said, 'It seems to me like you're showing all the classic symptoms of ADHD (Attention Deficit Hyperactivity Disorder). I'm going to go ahead and prescribe you some new medication to help you focus. I think this will help you a lot.'

No wonder I couldn't focus on anything and my brain was always going from one thought to another. No wonder I was always fidgeting and couldn't stay still. No wonder I was always late to everything.

Just as I did when I was diagnosed with OCD, I felt relief that came with a diagnosis.

*

One Spring day during my first year of college I got a text from Nick that changed everything:

Nick: *Hey*

Me: *Hey*

Nick: *I have a weird question for you.*

Me: *Yes?*

Nick: *Umm … would you ever … experiment with me?*

My heart fluttered and my throat closed up. Even though I had dreamed of it all this time, I had never thought it would actually happen.

Me: *Wait … so you're not straight?*

Nick: *I don't know.*

Me: *Does this mean you might like me?!*

Nick: *Maybe*

I was so happy, I felt like I was going to throw up. He *might* like me!

This was my chance. I would do anything to keep him around and get his love, and if that meant 'experimenting' with him, then so be it.

I jumped right from happiness and excitement to being nervous. I worried that this would change our relationship for the worse. But what if it turned into something more? Maybe Nick and I could become boyfriends.

I was also terrified because it would be my first time going further than making out with a guy. I didn't know what to do. Should I shave? Should I leave it as it is? Would he like my body? Or would he think it's gross? What if he thought I was a bad kisser? This was all so new to me and I didn't know how to feel.

I went home, changed into some nicer clothes, and sprayed on some cologne. And then, before I could talk myself out of it, I left for his house.

It was late, around midnight. His parents were sleeping, so I let myself into his house and walked into the basement, where I assumed he would be. And I was right. There he was, looking at me from the couch, looking just as nervous as I felt. I sat down next to him. There was a weird tension in the air. I could tell we were both feeling incredibly anxious.

'Hi,' I said.

'Hey,' he responded.

We stared at each other for a few seconds, neither of us not quite knowing what to do or how to start. I moved a little closer to him, and he moved a little closer to me. We locked lips and just like that, we were making out, something I had only dreamt about. I felt him caress my thigh and finger at my jean's button. This was happening. And there was no going back now. Not that I wanted it to end. I was all in.

For the first time ever, I felt connected to a guy in a whole new way.

Nick and I hooked up that night. That's the most detail I'm going to give you.

Walking back to my car, so many thoughts raced through my head, and to be honest, I was stunned and in disbelief about it all. For the first time ever, I believed I had a chance with him.

When I sat down in my car, I nearly jumped when my phone buzzed with a text from him.

Nick: *Sorry, I'm not gay. This never happened.*

Me: *So you don't like me?*

Nick: *Sorry, no. Delete these texts. This never happened.*

My heart was broken, once again. Even Nick, the person I idolized most in the world, had let me down. He never really liked me. He just used me to 'experiment'. I jumped into his arms, gave him my entire world, and he basically spat in my face. This may have 'never happened' for Nick, but it sure as hell happened for me. I sat in my car for what felt like an eternity and sobbed my eyes out.

I don't know how long I was there for before I started to feel an intense anger for Nick. Who was he to use me like this? Why would he mess with my heart like this? I felt an absolute hatred towards him, despised him.

I never wanted to see him again.

About a week after this happened, I lost my dream job at the veterinary clinic. I couldn't get myself out of bed before, let alone now after getting my heart broken. I laid in bed until the very last possible second and then dragged my body to work. I felt like dead weight rolling off my mattress. Driving to work, I was in a haze, everything felt foggy around me. One day, I walked into the clinic and my manager asked if we could go upstairs to talk. She took me into a room and the veterinarian who owned the place was there too, to my surprise. The moment I stepped into that room and saw him, I knew what was about to happen. My heart sunk and my breathing sped up. I began to lose control of my hands as they shook violently. She handed me a sheet of paper.

'This is a list of dates you were late and the number of minutes you were late by each day.'

'Oh. I see.' I could barely read the paper, because my hand was shaking so hard and my vision was blurred. I was lost for words. I had no idea what to say.

'We can't have someone working here who is this consistently late,' my manager said. 'We've given you plenty of warnings. We're going to have to let you go. Go collect your stuff and then I'll walk you out.'

I don't even remember walking out to my car. All I remember is sitting in the driver's seat once again, hyperventilating and crying.

Slowly but surely, my life was falling apart before my own eyes. And I couldn't do anything about it.

CHAPTER 3

It had been a long day. For hours, I had been sitting in a dim room with ugly green wallpaper, answering true and false questions about myself. All that was in the room was a white folding chair and table, and a psychiatrist's desk. I was ready to be done, and I wondered why they needed to know all of this useless information. Some of it seemed to make sense to form a diagnosis, but other questions just seemed simply dumb.

I find it hard to keep my mind on a task or a job. I checked the true box and skimmed down to the next line.

I would like to be a singer. Okay, I don't know what that has to do with anything.

No one seems to understand me. Very true.

At times I feel like smashing things. YES.

Evil spirits possess me at times. Um, no.

This was just one of the 26 tests that made up my diagnosis.

*

When Nick broke my heart, I completely shut down. I stopped going to school, dropped my classes, and just lay in bed all day. Nick and my friendship had ended, so I went back to his ex, Grace, and became close friends with her again. I graduated out of my theater group, a safe place of mine, and because of that,

I didn't really have an outside-the-family support system. I felt directionless and lonely and had no idea where I was going in life. I felt distant from everyone else and the world as a whole. I despised who I was as a person.

Meanwhile, my OCD had started to worsen more and more. I was continuing to count everything and check on things, but it became worse. My confessing got to its worst, and I would sit there in bed every day thinking about all of the 'horrible' things I've done, only to run to my parents and friends to confess. I no longer cared about controlling my thoughts, nor had the energy to do so. My thought process at the time was that it was just easier to give in.

Little by little, I lost all motivation I had to do anything. Every morning I woke up and felt limp and lifeless, as if all of the energy had been drained out my body. I began staying up until three or four in the morning, sleeping the entire day away. In other words, I became nocturnal.

I slept a lot, but somehow managed to feel tired and achy when I would wake up. It didn't make sense. I also stopped eating. It would register in my head that I was hungry and should probably eat something, but I wouldn't have the energy to get out of bed nor the motivation to get up. I would go all day without eating, only to get out of bed around 8pm and find a little something to eat. And when I did eat something, it usually wasn't the healthiest as I looked for the easiest thing to prepare.

For months, I was getting worse and worse, and it started to scare my loved ones. They wondered what was going on with me and were frightened as to why I was no longer living my life. I can imagine it was a horrible thing for them to watch and I was a terrible person to be around. I was never in a good mood and stopped partaking in family events. I never left my room and interacted with them, and when I did, I was in a horrible mood and would yell at them. I can't imagine how bad it was for them when my pale, skeleton-like body would leave the room only to scream at them.

For my family, it was obvious that we needed to find out what was going on, because they wanted me to get better. They wanted to see me happy and full of life again. So they made an appointment with a neuropsychological testing facility not too far from my house called NeuroHealth of Arlington Heights. My parents explained to me that this was important so that I could get better and be happy.

Finally, the day of the first appointment came.

Just like my initial evaluation with Diane so many years ago, it was a simple conversation with a psychologist that started this journey. She asked me questions about my daily habits, how I felt every day, my social life, and my fears. She then explained to me that they would be going forward with the neuropsychological testing.

'We will be administering over a dozen tests and evaluations to you over the next of month to see why you do the behaviors you do and the thoughts processes behind them,' she explained.

'Will I be diagnosed with something other than OCD and ADHD?' I asked.

'Most likely, yes,' she said.

I knew that a diagnosis meant hope of getting better. And I craved that.

But another part of me felt incredibly frustrated. *How many disorders could I possibly have? How crazy could I be?* I felt like there was so much to me that I just didn't know, and that scared me. That there might be more things inside me that were making me behave in the ways I was.

The first tests they administered to me were academic. I suppose they wanted to learn whether or not I have a learning disorder, as I've always had trouble with Math. I did a mix of Math problems and English / reading comprehension. As always, I had very low Math scores but excelled at reading and English.

These tests made me really anxious, even more than exams had made me feel in the past. I hesitated with every answer because I knew that the results of these tests were going to change my entire life. And I was tired of not knowing what was wrong with me.

Other tests involved completing puzzles with blocks, which I believe tested my hand-eye coordination and problem-solving ability. Other tests were obviously for memory, as I would have to remember certain patterns and shapes.

Throughout the tests, the psychologist would ask me a series of questions about my life or I'd be handed a page with questions on it that I'd have to fill out. I was never told where my answers went or what they meant.

One day, I came in and they set me up in front of a computer. They told me I had to press the spacebar every time I saw a certain number. So that's what I did for what felt like forever. I kept feeling an urge to leave, to just give up, say that I quit the test, but I was resolved to finish it, to find out what happened at the end. So I carried on, even though it felt like I was there for an entire lifetime, staring at the screen, just waiting for a number to come through so I could press the spacebar.

When I finished, the man with me during the test told me that it was to test my focus.

I thought this was pretty strange, because no one had ever told me the purpose of the tests before. I just had to figure it out myself.

'I probably did horribly because I have ADHD,' I said.

'Actually,' he said, 'you don't have ADHD. This test just pretty much confirmed that. Most likely, you have so much anxiety that it manifests itself as ADHD symptoms.'

This came as a huge shock for me. Here I was, thinking I had this disorder, that I had an explanation for some of my behavior, forming some of my identity around it, and they'd been completely wrong this entire time.

At the time, I didn't know how common it is to be misdiagnosed, that mental health takes time to understand. I was just confused.

The tests continued for a month. Eventually my report was ready to be released. One day, I got an email with my report, results of the tests attached. It was a little overwhelming at first, as it was 19 whole pages.

I cracked it open and began to read:

He reported significant feelings of self-doubt and low morale which contributes to various depressive feelings, thoughts, and behaviors throughout the day. Andrew expresses a mixed pattern of psychological problems which are localized within intense feelings of anxiety combined with self-doubting depression. Andrew is high strung and often worries to excess about most things. This worry causes inhibition in his responses to the world around him and can also result in withdrawal from participation in daily life.

I knew I had withdrawn from life, but it was really something to see someone else write it down and notice.

Andrew feels a distinct weight and burden by his need to achieve which is confounded by the aforementioned anxiety and depression. He tends to blame himself for his failures which causes him to become highly self-critical. This critical pattern does not conquer his underlying feelings of inadequacy, but merely compounds it further and further. Andrew's psychological distress, which leads to failures, psychomotor slowing, and elevated anxiety has caused him to develop a core self-belief of being less-than and inferior to others. Andrew has very little self-confidence and is assured of his own lack of achievement even prior to attempting to accomplish a goal. This has caused a general severe depressed mood for Andrew that is pervasive and strong. He feels guilty and unworthy, unhappy about his life, and deserving of punishment. Andrew's anxiety is high and he feels overwhelmed with anxiety about his future and his ability to contribute to society as a whole. Andrew's depression and anxiety has contributed to a lack of ability to navigate daily affairs and a retreat from the world. This has also resulted in subjectively perceived low memory and impairments in the completion of various simple daily living tasks. As such Andrew is immobilized and withdrawn, without the necessary energy for life.

Andrew can form very deep emotional attachments to others whom he feels may be his salvation. This causes him to be highly vulnerable to being harmed by others, even if their intent was not to be harmful. Andrew may blame himself for interpersonal problems experienced with others, whether or not he is generally at fault. While Andrew desires deep a meaningful connections with others, he is introverted and avoidant due to his feelings of inadequacy and vulnerability. He is likely shy and reclusive. Underlying these feelings of avoidance and distress is a keen sense of anger and resentment towards those whom he perceives have harmed him in the past. Andrew feels intense and unexpressed rage towards others which can cause him to be quietly critical of them, and wish revenge on them.

Andrew appears to lack the means for an autonomous existence and is especially vulnerable to separation anxieties and fears of desertion. This causes him an intense feeling of resentment towards those upon whom he depends. He will see them as harsh and misunderstanding critics of his life when they attempt to set boundaries or insure any level of growth or adjustment on Andrew's part. This resentment is oppressed within Andrew and he rarely, if ever, asserts these angry thoughts and feelings. He is often conciliatory and placating while harboring the aforementioned feelings. When Andrew feels overwhelmed by the requirements of daily living, which may happen often, he is unlikely to enlist the capacities within him to cope independently and instead turns to complaints of fatigue, weakness, or physical illness. Due to these intrapsychic difficulties, Andrew has some stunted development and is generally unsophisticated in his expectations, ideas, and impulses. Andrew views himself as childlike, weak, and vulnerable despite his age.

Finally, I got to the end:

The results of the social, emotional, and behavioral assessment reveal that a diagnosis of Obsessive Compulsive Disorder, Major Depressive Disorder, Chronic, Severe, and Borderline Personality Disorder are appropriate for Andrew at this time.

I sat there for the longest time, just staring at that final paragraph. I knew what depression was and I had started to suspect that I had it for a while. I felt like I was in a dark pit that I couldn't get out of, and depression had to be the only logical explanation for that. It explained so much.

Then my eyes swept over to 'Borderline Personality Disorder.' I had heard of it, but I had no idea what it was. I quickly picked up my phone and did a Google search, reading article after article about it, teaching myself about myself.

At first, I got that sense of relief that always came to me after a diagnosis. *Now I know what's going on and I can get better*, I thought.

However, during my research, my relief started to diminish. While I wanted to figure out how to get better, most of the articles out there had titles like 'How to Deal with Loved Ones with Borderline Personality Disorder.' There were barely any articles on how someone with Borderline Personality Disorder (BPD) could get better, only on how to be around people with this disorder. The phrase 'how to deal with' circled in my mind. *So that's who I am*, I thought. *Someone people have to 'deal' with*.

And then I came across the single worst word in an article: 'incurable.' And then I saw it in another. And another after that. My heart sank and I felt that familiar pain in my chest. The relief I'd had just minutes prior at the hope of recovery was now gone. According to the internet, I was never going to get better.

I'd be living like this for the rest of my life.

CHAPTER 4

It is three o'clock in the morning. I'm exhausted but I can't sleep. I'm too busy staring at the ceiling, picturing it caving in on top of me, instantly killing me. I think about how desperately I wish for this to happen. I am in my bed wrapped up in a large comforter, the only place where I truly feel safe. The only place where I truly want to be. The room is pitch dark, just how I like it. My thoughts swirl around in the void that is my brain.

My family would be better off without me.

My friends would be happy if I were dead.

Emma would feel horrible about what she did to me.

I can't take living anymore.

*

After my diagnosis, my life spiraled out of control in a whole new way.

The words 'incurable' and 'chronic' kept circling, never leaving me with any peace. Any hope of getting better was lost, so I just decided from that it wasn't even worth trying.

There's no point putting so much effort into something that'll never work. I'm forever crazy.

The only way I can describe depression is as a deep, dark, black hole that I can't escape from no matter how hard I try.

The air is thin and most of the time, I can barely breathe, like my throat has just closed up. I float around, desperately trying to hold onto anything solid, anything that will ground me, but I can't grasp anything. Once in a while, I might see a dim light in the distance, and I'll try my best to float towards it. But just as I get close, it extinguishes itself.

Many people think that depression is just another word for sadness, but I know that couldn't be further from the truth. Sadness you can escape from after some time. Depression is quite the opposite.

I was no longer in school. I lost all motivation to study or go to class, so I dropped all of them. My body constantly felt weak and shaky, like it was going to break at any second, and it was hard for me to even get out of bed to go to the bathroom, let alone go to class.

During that horrible year of my life, these were my typical days:

4am–12pm: Sleep

12pm–1pm: Stare at the ceiling

1pm–3pm: Put on some Netflix and drift in and out of sleep

3:30pm: Get up to use the toilet

4pm–6pm: Sleep, stare at the ceiling

7pm–8pm: Finally realize I'm hungry, try to muster up the motivation to get up

8pm: Finally get myself up out of bed to make a frozen pizza, the first thing I've eaten all day

8:30pm: Eat the entire frozen pizza by myself

9pm–4am: Alternate between watching Netflix and staring at the ceiling

This was pretty much the way every day passed when I wasn't with my friends. I tried to be with them as much as possible, to take a break from the dark cloud that I was living in.

Although people living with depression sometimes prefer to isolate themselves, I was quite the opposite. Friends became my coping mechanism. I was obsessed with them, constantly checking my phone to see if they had texted me or wanted to hang out. I wanted to be with them at all times. I hated being alone. I couldn't get myself out of bed for anything else, but the moment a friend texted me wanting to spend time together, I would jump out of bed and speed over to their house, excited to escape the pain that was overtaking me.

Each day felt like it was a week long, and I always felt as if they would never end. At times, I was completely overwhelmed by my emotions and it seemed as if I was feeling every single emotion in existence all at the same time. When that happened, I thought I was going to explode. Other times, all I felt was pure sadness. I cried at least once a day. Some days, I felt simply numb. At these times, I felt nothing inside of me. For someone who feels so deeply on a daily basis, these days were a sweet relief from the torture that went on inside of my head.

Living with me while I was in this state was not easy for my family, I'm sure. When they saw me daily, they had no idea what version of me they would get. Would they get the sweet and warm Andrew, the silent Andrew or the Andrew who snapped at them for no reason at all? I knew it made my mom feel unloved and my massive mood swings made her upset. She has told me about how worried this period of time made her and how it kept her up at night. I can imagine that the rest of my family felt the same way. I never wanted to spend any time with them, and when I was with them, I was just in a completely horrible mood. I don't think it could have made them feel very loved or wanted.

One day, my parents knocked on my door and told me that they had made an appointment for me to go see a new psychiatrist. Again, they had taken things into their own hands, made the decision for me.

I didn't argue with them at all this time. I desperately wanted help, some kind of medication, because I desperately wanted to get rid of the pain I was feeling inside of me. I didn't care if the medication made me feel numb or changed my personality, as many people told me it might. I didn't care that people told me I shouldn't be hooked on meds. All I cared about was not feeling the way I was anymore.

The day of the appointment came. I printed out the report about me with my diagnoses and headed over to the psychiatrist's office. After filling out a mountain of paperwork and waiting a good amount of time, a small lady greeted me at the door, smiled, and put out her hand.

'I'm Dr. Gupta, it's wonderful to meet you.'

She walked me over to a rather clean-looking office, weighed me, and had me sit in a leather armchair.

'Tell me about your family,' she said.

'Well ... we're pretty close and I would say I have a good relationship with them. But I'm not always the nicest to them. I've been yelling at them a lot lately and I haven't been spending time with them.'

'Why?'

'I spend all of my time in my room, or with friends.'

'Speaking of your friends, what is your social life like? Do you have many friends?'

'I have a good small group of friends. I spend a lot of time with them. It's the only thing that makes me happy and forget everything.

'Do you get along with them?'

'Well... we fight a lot. I get really jealous, and they say I'm really possessive and clingy.'

'Are you?'

'Yes. I am.'

'How about dating?'

'I haven't dated since I was 16. I want to but it's hard to meet other guys. Besides, I'm too busy with my friends.'

And so we went on, small questions that I had to answer about myself in order to find the solution. Just like it was with Diane all those years ago, I actually felt very comfortable sharing this personal information with her. She had a very comforting demeanor and I just wanted to share things with her. Plus, I knew that the information I shared would get me medication, and I desperately wanted that. I would do anything and share anything with her to get the meds.

Finally, came the moment of truth.

'Would you be comfortable with me prescribing you some type of medication?'

'Yes!'

And just like that, Dr. Gupta wrote me a prescription for meds. She explained to me that this pill that I would take on a daily basis would help limit the symptoms of depression, anxiety, and OCD.

'But what about my BPD?' I asked.

'Unfortunately, there is no medication for BPD. That will have to be treated with therapy. However, this medication will help lessen the anxiety that comes from your BPD, which may help you control it more.'

My heart sunk. When it came to the BPD, this furthered my evidence that there was no hope. The word 'incurable' that I had read so many times swallowed me up again.

I started taking the pills as prescribed, praying that they would work as promised. I needed some type of relief, desperately.

PART 4

ROCK BOTTOM

CHAPTER 1

During my stage of rock bottom, I was lucky to have some good friendships around me. For starters, I became friends with Nick again. With time apart, we both got over what had happened and remembered how good our friendship was.

But things weren't so simple as that. Our friendship, once again, became incredibly intense, and I sort of realized that the friendships I have with people are never truly going to be 'normal'. I attach too quickly, too intensely, and I demand too much of people.

My friendship with Nick also brought with it another close friendship with a person called Josh. Nick invited Josh around during one of our hangouts so I became friends with him as well. I had already known Josh for a while but we weren't close, at all. But when he started to hang out with me and Nick, we became very close. And Josh was already in a pretty serious relationship with one of my oldest friends, Charlotte. And so began our quartet, the three of them becoming the most important people to me outside of my family.

The routine was always the same. Every weekend, I would go over to Nick's house with an overnight bag. Josh would do the same, and Charlotte would come over too, but only for the evening. We would spend the Friday night together, eating food and playing games, and then Josh and I would spend the night at Nick's house, crashing on his couches. Nick and Josh and I would spend all of Saturday together, playing more video games and eating more food (a guy's dream), and then we would sleep over again at Nick's. Sometimes Charlotte would meet us later during the day. When we woke up on Sunday, we would spend the majority of that day together too, doing the same things. I pretty much lived at Nick's house every weekend. I even kept a toothbrush there.

This routine of living at Nick's house during the weekends became incredibly important to me. I always spent the weekdays in bed, being consumed by my own thoughts. The negative thoughts and my own emotions ate away at me, leaving me with no sense of peace. Being with people 24 / 7 during the weekends got me away from that and kept me distracted. For me, it was the perfect solution.

But it wasn't perfect for everyone. My parents were becoming more and more frustrated with me. My dad kept telling me that I had my priorities mixed up. What he meant was that I had previously focused on my future and my studies, yet now all that seemed to matter to me was hanging out with my friends as much as possible. He thought I had left my dreams of a future to the side to just be in the now.

But that wasn't the truth, not entirely. I didn't want to give up my dreams. If anything, they were making me feel even worse about myself. Because I knew I had been on the track for doing great things. I'd had a good job, was a student doing the course I wanted to do, had even won awards for my work. And now, everything felt like it had fallen away and there wasn't any possible way I could get it back.

And if my friends made me feel better during this time, then I was going to spend most of my time with them, even if it did make my parents frustrated and angry with me.

During this time, I realized something fundamental about myself and my relationships with my friends. I'd read that people who had BPD made very intense and strong friendships and that they would find themselves leaning on these friendships for validation in their lives. Which all sounded very familiar. But I also learned that people with BPD would focus on one person in their friendship group, putting a lot of interest and attention on them. The term for this person was Favorite Person, or FP for short.

Reading this, I realized that Emma and Nick had been my FPs in the past. I had put everything on them and when both of them had left me, it was absolutely heartbreaking. And now I knew why.

With Nick, Josh, and Charlotte, I had good friends but I didn't have an FP. And for a while, things were fine just like that.

But inevitably I found myself a new FP: Hunter. I'd known him since childhood, when I became good friends with his sister. When I first met him, he was just my friend's younger brother, nothing less, nothing more. But as both got older, Hunter and I started to become closer. He's incredibly handsome and has a winning personality, making him extremely popular. He's got it all: charm, a great sense of humor, and a dedication to those he loves. I've always seen him as the person who has it all together.

I'd definitely had FPs in the past, but Hunter was completely different. Everything about my relationship to him felt more intense. It wasn't just that he made me feel good when I was around him, though he did. It was like he became my life source. When I was away from him, even when I was with my other friends, I felt like there was a part of me that had been lost. He made me feel like I was good, like I was cured of everything, and I craved that. I wanted to feel like a good person. I wanted to feel whole again.

So, without either of us really talking about it, I started doing things for him just to keep him around. Whenever he was dating someone, I drove him around and constantly third-wheeled with his girlfriend. And I didn't even think about how they felt about me sitting in on their dates. I just wanted to spend time with him. I bought him expensive things without even asking, just showing up with something. I showered him with affection, complimenting him whenever I got the chance, never once thinking about how that made him feel. All I wanted was for him to validate me, to make me feel better, and to get there, I would do anything.

Over time, I realized that, just like Nick, I'd developed romantic feelings for him. In fact, I realized that I was completely in love with him.

Because I was so obsessed with him, I noticed every single thing that he did. And my mood wholly depended on what he was doing, how I felt he was treating me. One second, he'd give me attention and I'd feel like I was on top of the world, and the next he'd ignore me to talk to his girlfriend and I'd sit there, waiting for him to look back at me, feeling like the worst person in the world.

I became increasingly possessive and clingy, making him feel guilty for having other friends. I thought that if he truly cared about me, he would only want to spend all his time with me. I didn't realize how much I was to be around.

And the way I was to him in person was nothing compared to the way I treated him over text. Every time he did the tiniest, I would go into an intense rage. During these rages, I would get so angry that I couldn't even see, and my body would shake and convulse. I didn't care what I said to him when I was in one of these rages. All I cared about was getting my feelings out to him. I would often say things I didn't mean. These rages would happen at least a few times a week. Although I loved him so much, I would feel pure hate for him during these episodes, which was scary.

Something that often sparked this rage was Hunter not replying to my messages immediately. I'd instantly spiral into negative thoughts.

He's probably busy. Wait, maybe he's ignoring me? Oh my gosh, I'm annoying him. I hope he's okay, maybe he got hurt or something. Shit, he just liked something on Instagram, that means he's ignoring me. Why does he hate me so much? What did I do wrong? WHAT'S WRONG WITH HIM? Why doesn't he love me?! Why does he have to torture me like this?! FUCK HIM.

Me: *Hey*

Me: *Hello?*

Me: *???*

Me: *Where are you???*

Me: *Are you ignoring me?*

Me: *You're scaring me*

Me: *Please answer*

Me: *I know you're ignoring me, you were just on Instagram*

Me: *What the fuck?! Do you really hate me that much?!*

Me: *What did I do wrong?!*

Me: *Are you mad at me?!*

Me: *YOU KNOW WHAT. FUCK YOU. I HATE YOU. YOU DON'T CARE ABOUT ME AT ALL.*

Hunter: *Andrew, I was at church and couldn't really respond*

Me: *Oh ... I'm so sorry, please don't hate me, please forgive me, I'm so sorry I'll try better I'll do anything.*

Me: *I'm a horrible person. You probably hate me. I hate myself. I would understand if you didn't want to be friends anymore.*

These were the typical episodes I would have, usually while lying in my dark room, with nothing to focus on but my own negative thoughts and Hunter. They'd happen constantly, which I can only imagine was exhausting for Hunter.

And then later, after I'd calmed down, let the negative thoughts run their course, I'd begin to feel incredibly guilty and start to panic that he was going to start disliking me. I would sit there beating myself up, wishing I could undo what I had just done. The constant shame was terrible. I'd convince myself that I was a horrible person who deserved to be punished.

*

It's three in the morning. Per usual, I am lying in my bed, just staring at the ceiling and thinking about life. I feel unloved. I feel lonely. I feel alone and misunderstood. I am seething at how much I hate myself.

I get up and creep to the kitchen, trying not to wake up my family. My body feels sore, like I've been running all day, and my ears have a faint ringing sound in them. My head feels like it's about to explode and my heart beats fast. I sit at the kitchen table and silently sob into my hands, being careful not to be too loud. Finally, I muster the strength to get out of that chair and pick up one of the long steak knives we have in our kitchen. I stand there with the knife to my wrist, desperately trying to talk myself into slitting it, with the intention of ending my life.

I don't want to be here anymore. It would be better for everyone. It would hurt, but it would still be better than feeling the pain I'm feeling inside now.

Then I think of my parents. I think of my siblings. I think of Hunter. And I put the knife down and go back to my room to finish sobbing.

Unfortunately, this wasn't the first or last time that happened.

Over time, spending more and more time in my bed, with increasing social problems, my thoughts became more and more sinister.

I would lie in my bed and Google the best ways to end your life. I'd read and read and read, trying to muster up the energy to get myself to do it. I would picture killing myself and would imagine how my family and friends would react. I would imagine them crying at my funeral, and vividly daydream about the conversations they would have about me.

The suicidal thoughts would come throughout the day. The moment I was alone, they'd arrive to keep me company. They would be at their strongest after I had episodes with Hunter, because I felt so bad, I thought I deserved to die. Not only that, but I began to use suicide as a manipulation technique with Hunter. For example:

Me: *You wouldn't even care if I died.*

Hunter: *Of course I would!*

Me: *I could kill myself right now and you wouldn't even care*

Hunter: *How could you even say that?! Of course I would care!*

Me: *Maybe I'll do it. I know you'd be happy.*

My manipulation and intensity of conversations with Hunter became progressively worse. I began to try and control him more, using the worst things possible to send him on guilt trips, to twist his emotions. I turned every single conversation towards me. I hungered for it.

I knew manipulation was a big part of BPD, and I knew it was bad, but I couldn't stop myself. I couldn't control myself, so I wanted desperately to control something.

CHAPTER 2

'I think everyone would be better off without me. All I am is a burden to my family and friends.'

'Andrew, let's try to reframe those thoughts,' Diane said.

'No, it's true.' I started to tear up. 'If I were gone, everyone would be happier.'

'Andrew.'

'I don't want to do this anymore. I don't want to be alive.'

'Andrew, at this point I don't feel comfortable letting you leave this session for your own safety. We either need to call your parents and tell them what is going on or call an ambulance.'

'No! I'm not going to actually kill myself. It's okay.'

'Andrew, I told you, we either call your parents or an ambulance. You choose.'

I felt pure rage at Diane. Here was someone I had trusted since I was nine years old. Why would she do this to me? All I was trying to do is share my feelings.

'Fine. We'll call my parents.'

We called my dad. He was with my mom and put the call on speaker phone. Diane explained to them what I'd told her and that she was concerned for my own personal safety. She tells them that I shouldn't be alone. They agreed to watch me overnight and take me to the hospital in the morning to be evaluated for inpatient or outpatient hospitalization.

Before I left the office, out of anger towards Diane, I said, 'So what's to stop me from climbing up a building on the way home and jumping off?'

'Andrew, I'm trusting that you won't do that,' she said. I knew that as much as I wanted to jump off a building on the way home, I cared enough about Diane to make sure I didn't let her down.

On the way home, I started sobbing. I was crying so hard that it was beginning to be difficult for me to drive, so I pulled over into a parking lot. *How can this be happening? How did I get to this point? What's wrong with me?!*

I pulled out my phone.

Me: *Hunter, my therapist is worried for my safety. I might be hospitalized tomorrow. I'm so scared.*

Hunter: *Andrew, take some deep breaths and try to calm down. Everything's gonna be okay.*

Me: *No it's not. I'm so crazy I might be put into a psych hospital. I'm crazy.*

Hunter: *No you're not. Maybe this is what you need to get better. God's in control.*

I fixated on those last few words. God is in control. God is in control. God is in control.

I wiped the tears out of my eyes, closed them, folded my hands, and began to pray for the first time I could remember.

'God,' I said. 'Please be with me. I need you. I can't do this alone.'

And just like that, I drove home, anticipating what was to come.

*

The next morning, my dad and I pulled up to the psych hospital, about a half hour away from my house, an overnight bag in my lap. This was the same hospital I'd first come to 11 years ago to start my therapy with Diane. We walked inside and I went up to the lady at the desk.

'Hi, I would like to be evaluated.'

She handed me a huge stack of forms without saying anything. *Of course*, I thought.

The forms ranged from insurance information to questionnaires on my sleeping patterns. Eventually, my eyes found the statement 'I want to end my life.' Without hesitating, I checked the 'Yes' box.

I handed the forms in and then sat there, waiting for quite a while.

Inevitably, they eventually called out my name. A woman smiled at me and pointed me towards a room down the hallway. It was exactly like the room Diane had brought me to all those years ago for my first evaluation session. Small, kind of stuffy, with two green plastic couches and a coffee table in the middle.

'How are you?' she asked.

'I'm kind of nervous.'

'That's understandable,' she said. 'I'm just going to ask you some questions. Let's start with what you're diagnosed with.'

'OCD, generalized anxiety, Major Depression Disorder, and Borderline Personality Disorder.' I rattled them off like I was ordering a sandwich.

'What does a typical day look like for you and how many hours of sleep do you get a night?'

'Well ... I usually don't go to bed until around 4am. I spend most of the day lying in bed and sleeping. I don't usually eat anything until nighttime.'

'Okay, I see. Have you ever wanted to hurt anyone else?'

'No ... Well, between you and me, sometimes I fantasize about hurting other people my friends spend time with, but I would never actually do it.'

'Okay. Have you ever thought about hurting yourself or ending your life?'

'Yes.'

'Do you have current plans to do so?'

'No … But I think about it most of the day. I've looked up ways to kill myself. And to be honest, sometimes when I get into one of my moods, I worry about what I would do … I get very impulsive when I'm upset and I'm afraid of what I might do should I get out of control.'

'Okay, Andrew. You can go back out to your dad and we'll call you back in shortly.'

I left the room and quietly sat back next to my dad in the waiting room. It wasn't too long before she called me back into the room.

'Okay, Andrew. We're going to suggest you stay here for a little while in our inpatient hospital. We feel that it's important for your own safety to get you stabilized, to watch you while we adjust your medication, because you're not caring for yourself. You won't be able to have your phone while hospitalized, so I suggest that you contact those important to you right now before it is taken away. I'm going to have you wait with your dad a little longer while we get approval from your insurance company.'

My heart dropped into my stomach. I knew that this was a likely scenario, but for some reason, I thought that there was always hope that it wouldn't happen. I mean, I definitely wasn't as bad as most people, right? All of a sudden, I started shaking. *This is not happening to me. I'm not crazy. I'm fine, normal. I'm not broken. I'm not wrong.*

I left the room and right away went and told my dad. Then I stepped into the hallway and called my mom.

'I love you. Everything's going to be okay,' she said.

I texted Charlotte, Josh, and Nick. They told me they loved me and that everything was going to be okay. They told me that they were there if I needed anything at all. I hadn't told them the truth of what was going through my head. They knew I didn't really do anything other than hang out with them but they didn't know the true extent of my problems. I think hearing this shocked them.

Then I texted Hunter. I debated about it for a while, going back and forth with myself. I wanted to tell him where I was. But he had just broken up with his long-term girlfriend a few days ago and I felt horrible about leaving him, about making him worry about me, about making myself the center of attention. But I knew I had to tell him, that I couldn't just leave him in the dark about what was happening with me. He told me that he loved me and that everything would be okay, just as most people were telling me.

After texting everyone I needed to, I sat for a little bit longer and was eventually called back into that tiny room. My dad was invited back in as well. I had a couple of forms to sign. First, they had me sign something saying that I wasn't going to be able to purchase a firearm for a certain amount of years. Next, I had to sign something saying that I was voluntarily admitting myself into the hospital. Yes, this was all voluntary; but I knew it needed to be done in order to get better. Both me and my family had discussed it. The last thing I needed to sign was a form that asked should I get out of control, how I would like to be restrained. How crazy did they think I was?! It had the option of some kind of sedative being injected into me or being locked into a room by myself to calm down. I checked the box that allowed me to be locked into a room. Not that it would ever happen, I knew.

I then sat in the waiting room for about another 45 minutes while they waited for approval from our insurance company. They explained to me that should they give approval, I would likely be approved for five through ten days. This was around the time that most people stayed in this particular hospital, as their goal in inpatient care was merely stabilization. Eventually, they called me in and said that the insurance company had approved me for eight days. Should they feel like I need longer, they explained, they would again contact the insurance company.

Before I knew it, my dad was handing me my overnight bag and it was time to say goodbye. I gave him a hug, and he reassured me that he loved me and would see me soon. Then the lady said, 'Alright, you can either give your phone to me now or you can give it to your dad.'

I panicked. I was horribly addicted to my phone. It was my lifeline because, without it, I would be without all of the people I so desperately depended on, especially Hunter. I thought about not being able to see them, let alone speak to them, all week and started to panic. *They're going to forget about me*, I thought. *They're all going to hang out without me. They're going to realize how wonderful it is without me and then they're going to leave me.*

But I knew I had to give it over to them, that I had to let this thing go. Reluctantly, I handed over my phone.

A man came to walk me upstairs to the inpatient part of the hospital. It was time.

*

We took an elevator upstairs, and he used a keycard to get into the ward. The doors slammed behind us. I was officially locked in: there was no leaving until they told me I could. He took me into another small room, but this time it was an exam room. He had me strip down to my underwear and put on a paper gown. He then took all of my clothes and slipped them into a plastic bag. He asked me to step onto the scale.

'105 pounds,' he said.

The weight shocked me. It was probably because I barely ate. Clearly, this was not a healthy weight for a 5ft-4in 20-year-old boy.

'Okay, I'm gonna need you to slip off your underwear and lift your gown for me to see.'

Wow, this is what I've been reduced to, I thought. Embarrassed, I did what he asked.

'Now turn around so I can see the other side. Then you can put your underwear back on.'

I did as he asked, becoming increasingly red in the face.

'Why did I need to do that?' I asked, slipping my boxers back on

'We needed to make sure you're not trying to smuggle anything in you can use to hurt yourself or others.'

After taking my blood, a different nurse came and brought me to another room. I was still wearing my paper gown. She was a kind-looking lady who seemed to make me feel calm as soon as she walked into the room.

'When will I get my clothes back?' I asked.

'We need to go through them first and make sure everything is in order. You should have them back in the next few hours. It's okay, everyone has to walk around in the gown when they first get here.'

Next few hours?! They expected me to walk around in this paper gown for hours, with my boxers for the whole world to see?!

'We're just going to have you sign a few more forms,' she said. I could tell she was hesitating, about to say something. '... So you don't want to be alive?'

Wow, that was not subtle at all. 'No, I don't.'

'Why not?' she asked.

'I'm a burden to everyone I know. All I do is mess up and disappoint others. My family and friends would be better off without me. The world would be better off without me. I'm certain of it.'

'You know you won't feel that way forever, right? Pain is always temporary. Think about what you were sad about two years ago, are you still sad about that today? You're going to get better, you know. I believe in you.'

I had never really thought about it that way. It had always felt like pain was permanent, never to leave. For the first time in a very long time, that lady made me feel a little bit of hope. Hope that I would one day recover and live a happy life.

She handed me my schedule. She explained that there were different group sessions throughout the day, with different topics to teach us various coping methods. This is what the schedule looked like:

8am: Wake Up / Hygiene

8:45am: Breakfast

9am: Morning Medication

9:30am: Community / Goals / Mindfulness

10:30am: Group session

11:30am: Expressive therapy

12:30pm: Lunch

1:15pm: Group session

2:00pm: Depending on the day it was either mass, visiting or expressive therapy

3:00pm: Free time or gym (staff permitting)

4:00pm: Group session

5:00pm: Staff check-in

5:30pm: Dinner

6:30-7:30pm: Either visiting or group session

8:00pm: Processing goals

9:00pm: Free time

10:30pm: Bedtime

Phone times were 7am–9:30am, 12:30pm–1:15pm, 5pm–6:30pm, and 9pm–10pm. I looked at the schedule and was a bit overwhelmed.

We're all adults, why can't we do what we want? Really, we have a bedtime?

Right away, I knew this schedule was going to be extraordinarily hard for me. I was used to staying up until 4am and sleeping in until the late afternoon. I was also accustomed to short naps throughout the day. I wasn't even used to three meals a day, just one large one at night. I knew getting adjusted was going to be tricky.

'I'll show you your room.'

Outside of the room was a nursing station where a variety of different nurses were sitting at computers. Phones lined the main room, with two small rooms filled with tables and televisions coming off it. I followed her down a hallway, until we reached Number 106. We went inside.

The room was very different from the padded room I'd expected. The dark room contained two beds, two desks, an armchair, and two nightstands. I noticed that all of the furniture was nailed into the ground, probably for our own protection. There was a small bathroom in each room, with a sink, shower, and toilet.

She handed me a pink plastic bin with a toothbrush, a comb, a washrag, a body towel, toothpaste, body wash, shampoo, deodorant, and some Vaseline.

'Here's everything you need,' she said to me. 'If you run out of something or need anything at all, let someone at the nursing station know. Breakfast starts at 8:45am tomorrow. Well ... I'll leave you to it.' And just like that, she left the room and I was alone.

I had never felt more alone than I did at that exact moment in that small, dark room. The second she left, I started crying.

I went over and looked at myself in the bathroom mirror. I barely recognized myself. Here I was, some pale, skinny person who had dark patches underneath his red eyes. I looked down the collar of my paper gown to see the ribs protruding through my skin. I looked like a skeleton. I didn't know how I had become this, how I had let myself be this person.

'Hi.'

I practically jumped out of my skin and quickly rubbed the tears out of my eyes. I turned around. There, standing and staring at me, was just some normal-looking guy. He looked to be around my age, with brown Justin Bieber-style hair, fairly tall, and beautiful green eyes. He was wearing brown sweatpants, a white undershirt, and the hospital-issued socks. I glanced down and saw that just like me, he was wearing a laminated wristband around his wrist which surely meant he was a patient here as well. I was surprised. I thought everyone here would be so much older than me, but here was someone who was young just like me. He looked ... normal, not someone I would expect to see in a mental institution.

'Hi,' he said again. 'I'm Jeremy.'

'Hi, nice to meet you,' I said. 'I'm Andrew.' We both glanced over to the door as a nurse peeked her head into the room, surely doing one of her 15-minute checks.

'Bedtime's in 15,' she said and then left.

'I'm your roommate, you can have that bed over there. I have the one by the window. I'm new to this place too, just got here this morning. Don't worry about the gown I had to wear that my first few hours too, you'll get your clothes soon.'

'Thanks, I can't wait to get out of this and into real clothes.'

'So what're you in for?'

I wasn't sure if I wanted to tell him, but what was I supposed to do? Lie? I quickly learned that in the psych hospital, you get to know people very fast.

'Ummm ... suicidal thoughts ... wasn't taking care of myself ... that kinda stuff." I looked down at my feet

'Yeah, I'm here for suicide stuff too. Literally had a gun to my head this morning when Mom found me and took me here. You a first timer? I am. It seems like everyone here has been here multiple times.' He spoke fast, like he couldn't keep the words in his mouth.

'Yeah, it's my first time here.'

'We'll be okay. At least we're in it together,' he said. 'So what you got? I have bipolar.'

I paused for a moment before answering. 'Uh, I have BPD.'

'Oh nice, that's kinda like bipolar in a way.'

A nurse peeked her head into the room again. 'Lights out, gentlemen.'

We both climbed into bed, which was quite hard under me, and I wasn't the most comfortable seeing as I was still wearing a paper gown. Jeremy and I continued to talk for hours that night about both of our mental illnesses and what it was like to live with them, pretending to sleep every time a nurse looked into the room. For the first time ever, I was talking to someone who truly understood what it was like to be me and that felt amazing. I related to him in so many ways, and he knew what it was like to walk in my shoes.

'Goodnight man, it's good to have a friend in here,' he said.

'Goodnight,' I said. 'It's nice not to feel so alone anymore.'

CHAPTER 3

That night I had an incredibly hard time sleeping, tossing and turning. I just couldn't go to sleep, no matter how hard I tried, and before I knew it, the nurses were waking us up.

'Breakfast!' they yelled into our room.

And I didn't get up. I was too tired and not motivated to get out of bed, as usual. Technically, I had signed a sheet saying I would participate in all activities and meals, but they didn't force you to do so. So I took advantage of that and stayed in my bed almost the whole first day. I didn't go to any of the sessions once in the morning for them to take my vitals (which they did every morning). Meanwhile, Jeremy went to most of the sessions, so I was left alone in my room. He would come check on me once in a while and urge me to come to session with him, but every time he did, I told him I just didn't feel like it and he didn't push it any further.

Finally, when lunch rolled around, I was getting too hungry to sit in the bed anymore. It had been 24 hours since I'd last eaten. I got up and noticed that they had left my clothes stuffed in a pillowcase on my dresser. Finally, I was able to get out of that paper gown. I went through my sack, and quickly noticed that they didn't include everything I had brought. My sweatshirt was gone and so were a pair of my sweatpants. I later learned that this was because they had strings in them which I could use to hurt myself if I wanted to. I slipped on a pair of the sweatpants that they did let me have and a T-shirt and shuffled out of the room towards the dining room.

'Andrew,' one of the nurses said when she saw me. 'You weren't at breakfast, so you weren't able to pick out what you wanted for lunch. We picked something out for you. Make sure you fill out the menu on your tray and turn it in so we can know what you want for dinner.'

I picked up my tray, which had a Coke, a bag of chips, and a plate covered by a top on it. I walked into the dining area and looked around, not knowing where to sit. Most of the tables were filled, not that I really wanted to interact with anyone anyway. I looked around for Jeremy and my heart sunk when I saw that his table was filled. I saw an empty chair over at one of the corner tables and took my chance with an old lady. 'Um ... can I sit here?' I asked.

'Of course, sweetie!' She beamed at me with a pair of pearly white teeth. 'I'm Barbara.'

'Hi, I'm Andrew, nice to meet you.'

'Did you just get here last night?'

'Yes, how long have you been here?'

'It's been six days now. But I'm getting out this afternoon!'

I wondered if I would be there for six whole days. This was a hospital where people stayed two weeks or less, just to get them grounded and safe. They wanted their patients to basically step back off the ledge before they left.

I looked around at the rest of the table. There was an old man sitting across from me who looked like he was half asleep. Looking down, I saw that his arm was bandaged all the way up to his elbow. I wondered if that was the reason why he was here. Next to him was a young Hispanic girl, who was quietly staring down at her plate. Next to her was a middle-aged man with a long beard, rocking back and forth in his seat while enjoying his pasta. Next to him was another girl who looked to be around my age, with long black hair. She looked up at me and smiled, and I noticed that her teeth were broken and brown.

I lifted the cover off of my plate and saw a plate of mostaccioli. It actually looked pretty good, and I was really surprised to learn that it also tasted delicious. I picked up the menu next to my plate and tried to choose something for dinner. There were far more options than I thought there would be. I was thrilled to notice that they had given me a special vegetarian menu. I decided to go with the side salad, a vegetable stir-fry, a lemonade, and a brownie. The food in the hospital was actually amazing. It was nice to be able to pick good food from such a variety of options.

I spent the rest of that first day in my bed, only coming out for dinner. I had heard that most people spend the first day in their room, but soon get acclimated to the hospital. I decided that the next day, I would try. If anything, the food was good enough to get me out of bed in the morning.

I woke up the next day to a lady standing over my bed.

'I'm Cheryl, your caseworker,' she said. She was a kind-looking lady with blue eyes and a blonde bob. 'Do you mind if we take a few moments to chat?'

We walked out of the room to a pair of armchairs and sat down. She asked me how I was doing, how I was getting acclimated, if I'd had any crying spells, what my mood had been like, and if I'd been thinking about hurting myself since I'd gotten there. She encouraged me to go to as many sessions as I can, as the more I went to and the more I was involved with everything, the more likely I was to get out sooner. I would end up meeting with her a few times during the stay at the hospital.

After a great breakfast of French toast, orange juice, and oatmeal, I sat down for our first group session. A large man in a polo slapped a sheet of paper down in front of me. The sheet asked us to list the recovery tasks we'd be working on that day, three things we can do to work on those tasks, and the process issue we wanted to bring up to group today. It also asked us to rate our mood, sleep, appetite, and energy. They asked us to fill out the sheet, and then wanted a few of us to share with the room some of our answers. Then someone would bring up their process question such as 'I'm feeling lonely today, what should I do?' And the rest of the room would talk that out with the person.

This was our daily after-breakfast routine. At the end of every day after dinner, we would have a group session where we reflected on our day and talked about how we accomplished our goals. Scattered throughout the days were individual sessions on a variety of coping topics. Some of the ones I found most helpful for me were boundaries, self-esteem, journaling, anger management, communication, anxiety management, and conflict resolution. At the time, I had no positive coping methods. All my coping methods I knew were detrimental to my life. This was the first time I had ever learned that there was a different, more healthy way to managing my depression and BPD.

But though I was learning things that were going to help me deal with what I had, the thing I looked forward to the most out of every day. Being away from my friends was causing me massive amounts of anxiety and I couldn't stop myself from thinking about what they might be doing without me. On the first day, after calling my parents, I asked them to go into my phone so I could jot down some of my friends' numbers. Of course, after talking to my parents, the first friend I called was Hunter ... I had his number memorized. In fact, I tried to call him every day, which considering the amount of time I was in the hospital, was a little much. He didn't always answer, but we did talk a couple of times. One day, I decided to call Nick, and was thrilled to learn that he was currently with Josh.

'Hi Nick!'

'How're you doing, buddy?'

'I'm okay ... It's very boring in here. Hey, visitations are tomorrow, would you want to come and see me?'

And just like that, Nick and Josh agreed to come visit me in the hospital! I was so excited. They would be able to give me and update on what was going on with my friends in the outside world and I wouldn't have to go all of this time without seeing them. I was counting down the minutes.

Meanwhile, I was learning more coping mechanisms and making new friends. I was getting closer and closer to Jeremy and, during free time, was beginning to sit and talk with other patients.

One of the more frustrating group sessions was expressive therapy, an art form of therapy. My first expressive therapy, we sat in a circle with maracas and bongo drums, playing different beats and singing a song. I felt like an idiot. A lot of the people seemed to enjoy it, but all it did was cause me anxiety. How was this supposed to help anyone?

A middle-aged looking lady with straight, long black hair beckoned me next to her.

'It's stupid, right? Wanna get out of here?'

'Yes, please!'

We walked out of the room and headed over to the other common room. We sat down at a table with a stack of coloring sheets and crayons on it.

'I'm Deborah,' she said. 'I'm gonna show you how to survive in here.'

It turned out that Deborah was a depressed, drug-addicted attorney who had been in the same hospital four times. I met so many people in the psych ward, from nurses, to businessmen, to retired veterans, to school teachers. But Deborah was special, and she became my best friend in the ward. We ended up spending most free-times together, sat together during most group sessions, and ate together at most meals. She made the hospital tolerable.

Eventually, I was assigned a hospital psychiatrist, and he prescribed me a new medication, Zoloft, and also something to help me sleep. He explained that I was expected to go to the medication window to receive my medication, and that I was to let them know if I was experiencing any of the side effects.

Slowly but surely, the first visitation day came. They ended up opening the doors 15 minutes late. I was pissed. We only had an hour for our visit, and I was splitting that up between my parents, and Nick and Josh. I had a wonderful time with my parents and friends telling them what it was like to be inside of the hospital and catching up with them. But when it was time for them to go, I thought of Deborah, who always told me to stand up to the nurses. I stood up and said to the nurse loudly so everyone could hear:

'You opened the doors 15 minutes late. We deserve an extra 15 minutes. I only got 15 minutes with my friends and that's not fair.' I felt scared saying it but stood my ground, waiting for a response.

After a second, I got a response: 'Fine, you get your extra 15 minutes.'

Everybody cheered and said thank you to me after that visitation, and it felt amazing to stand up for myself, despite my anxiety.

One night they let us watch a movie, and that was a great night. Me and my fellow patients talked, bonded, and had so many laughs. Even the nurses got in on it. It was a wonderful time. Somehow, I never thought I would enjoy myself in the hospital but I had some very enjoyable moments. However, that night, when I got back to my room, I found a little piece of paper underneath my bin. It was from Jeremy. We had spent every night I had in the hospital so far having deep talks and often sat together at lunch. We had made each other feel normal.

Andrew, I was discharged. I'm sorry I didn't get to say goodbye. Thank you for being such a good friend in this place. Please contact me anytime if you need support or to talk. – Jeremy

Underneath Jeremy's name was his phone number. Exchanging contact information or even last names was totally against the rules in this place, which is why he'd hid the note underneath my bin. I went to read the phone number and my heart sunk. The last four digits of the number were blurred out by a water stain. Till this day, I still wonder how Jeremy is doing and what he is up to. I really hope he is doing well.

The next night was Super Bowl Sunday and everyone was sitting in the common room excitedly, waiting for the game to start. A nurse walked in.

'Hey everyone! We have a surprise for you. In honor of the Super Bowl, we brought up pizzas and dessert. Help yourself!' In the hospital, the tiniest things can make you happy and this seemed to brighten up the whole evening. It was another great night of bonding and surprisingly good pizza.

I spent the next few days going to group and doing everything that I was supposed to do, just as they asked me to do it. Eventually, my psychiatrist called me in and let me know that he thought I was stable enough to go home.

It was funny, but although I was pretty excited to leave, I also didn't want to leave. It felt amazing to be in the hospital. I was the calmest I'd ever been in my life, stranded here, away from all my triggers. It turned out, even though I had only been there for under two weeks, I was actually terrified to leave. When I left, I wouldn't have the support I had there. I would go back to no one understanding me. I would have to try and cope on my own, using the skills I had been taught.

But I had to leave. I couldn't stay in the hospital forever.

So I called my mom and let her know I was allowed to leave. I filled out my discharge paperwork, which was one of the requirements before they let me go. I was also required to fill out a detailed after-care plan, which included outpatient hospitalization, personal therapy, and continuation of medication. I was also had to describe in detail what skills I would use should I become triggered and / or suicidal.

My caseworker visited me and let me know that my after-care plan would be outpatient hospitalization, in which I would come to the hospital for group sessions Monday–Friday for a couple of months but be allowed to sleep at home. It was a pretty good deal, I thought, and made me feel better that I wouldn't be completely on my own yet.

The last thing I did before I left was say goodbye to Deborah. I was sad to say goodbye to her, as I didn't know if I would ever see her again. I went into the group she was in, which was an expressive therapy group, where they were drawing pictures of trees. I went over, sat next to her, and began drawing my own tree. The therapist in the room explained that our trees represented who we were inside. *Bullshit*, I thought. This is why I hated expressive therapy.

'I'm getting discharged in the next few minutes. Goodbye, Deborah, thank you for everything,' I whispered to her.

'You are a wonderful person, Andrew. I really wish you the best. I know you will get better. I have so much hope for you.'

She took my tree, slyly folded over the edge of the paper, and wrote down her phone number with a colored pencil.

I walked out of the room and they handed me the duffel bags with my belongings. I stripped my bed and changed out of my sweatpants into jeans and a sweater. A man walked me down to my mom's car and, as we drove away, I looked back at the hospital, feeling both happy and sad to be leaving.

CHAPTER 4

I spent two days away from the hospital and tried to use as many coping skills I'd learned as I possibly could. I quickly learned that when you are actually in the moment, using your coping skills is not as easy as they make it sound. For one, when you're overwhelmed with emotion, it's very hard to think clearly enough to start a coping skill. Also, when someone is in recovery, it's often difficult to know when you're actually doing something wrong. To a person with mental illness, their behavior is perfectly normal, because they live with it daily. They're so used to what they do, it's hard to know that they're doing anything out of the ordinary. It takes therapy and dedication to learn healthy behaviors.

I found it incredibly hard being away from the hospital for those two days. My anxiety went through the roof the moment I got my phone back and was connected with my friends again, as my triggers were once again prevalent. It may seem weird, but for a long time after leaving inpatient care, I missed it and wanted to go back. I craved the calmness, support, and understanding I felt while living there. Sometimes I even crave that environment up until this day.

As I knew it would, the day came where I needed to start my outpatient hospitalization. For the next couple of months, I would be spending all day every Monday–Friday in group therapy.

Every night, we were required to fill out a sheet to list our goals for the day and track our moods, appetite, and sleep. There was one box for whether you'd had suicidal thoughts that day and one that asked whether you had a plan in place. Almost every day that first month and a half, I checked that I had suicidal thoughts but did not have a plan. On Friday nights, we were given a sheet to plan for our weekends. During these weekends, we were without the support of the hospital, so it was important to plan how we would cope during those two days.

The first group session of every day was sharing time. Although there was a therapist present for facilitating, us patients pretty much ran the group ourselves. My first day, I walked into the room late because I was busy signing paperwork, which unfortunately made everyone look at me. I was super happy to see that I recognized some faces from when I was an inpatient and that I wouldn't have to start from scratch in making friends. I sat down and the therapist began.

'So, as many of you know, each day we begin by sharing the rules of this program. Would someone please start?'

'No touching,' someone blurted out.

'No sharing contact information or last names,' someone else said.

'If you see someone from the program out in the real world, you are not to acknowledge that you know them.'

'Everything said in group stays in group.'

'Use I-statements.'

It seemed like there were so many rules in this hospital, and it seemed very hard to remember all of them. However, by the end of it all, I was a pro and became one of the people blurting out rules.

'Now,' the therapist said, 'who wants to bring up their process question?'

Silence. For what felt like forever. Everyone sat there twiddling their thumbs and staring down at their feet. Finally someone spoke: 'I feel like my mom doesn't understand my depression. Yesterday she told me to "just get over it", and that made me feel really devalued. Does anyone have any advice on this?'

More silence, until after what felt like hours someone finally spoke. Then another few minutes of silence until someone else spoke. This is what group sharing was like, and I often had this once or twice a day. It was a session I had every morning, and twice a week with a group of millennials exclusively. I never did bring up my own process question, but it still helped me. Although sometimes I didn't relate to the problem, a lot of the times I realized that these people and I were not so different. We were going through much of the same stuff. Just as it did in inpatient, it felt amazing to be validated in this way.

After the second session of the day was lunchtime. They handed us all a red lunch ticket and we headed over to the cafeteria to eat. Once again, the food didn't disappoint. Just as I did in inpatient, I eventually found a group of friends to sit with every day. These fellow patients ranged from my age to older people, but we were all bonded through our shared experiences, so age didn't really matter. Once again, I met people of all professions. Students, flight attendants, salesmen. No matter who you are or what your situation is, mental illness does not discriminate.

Because my sleeping schedule was still so messed up, I had a hard time getting to the hospital on time every day, so as a result, I was pretty much late almost every day the first month. Eventually, they pulled me aside and had me sign a contract that I would be on time from now on or I would be dismissed from the program. I wanted help, so from that moment on I worked on adjusting my sleeping schedule to one that is healthy.

I learned that the hospital taught 12 basic coping skills to help us when we were out.

1. Grounding

2. Thought Stopping

3. Reality Check

4. Reframing

5. Positive Self-Talk

6. I-Statements

7. Assertiveness

8. Boundaries

9. Deep Breathing

10. Visualization

11. Thought Log

12. Journaling

Along with these, we were encouraged to try and change our negative core beliefs about ourselves (like how I thought I was a horrible person) and reframe our thoughts. We also learned about what thoughts are rational and what are irrational. With mental illness, it can be very hard to know when your brain is lying to you. Learning how to make the difference is very important.

For one talk, they had a nutritionist come in to talk to us about our diets and how important they were to both our physical and mental health. She went through the various vitamins and minerals and what we should be consuming daily. It was at that point that I realized how malnourished I was. I definitely wasn't getting all of my required vitamins and minerals, and I was definitely way too underweight. After all, on average, I ate about one meal a day. And that one meal was whatever I could make the fastest so I could get back into bed. I decided from then on that I would try and eat all three meals a day and eat healthier. As the nutritionist said, 'a healthy diet is a healthy brain,' and I desperately wanted to do anything I could to get better.

The last session of every day was always expressive therapy, which I absolutely hated. I've never been an artsy person, and expressive therapy seemed to do the opposite of what it was meant to do and caused me more anxiety. We were required to switch days: one in the gym and the next in the art room. However, I would break the rules and just go to the art room every day. Because even though I hated the expressive therapy, I hated the gym more. The whole thing was very triggering for my OCD. The smell, sweat, and possible germs made it impossible for me to enjoy any kind of activity in the gym. One time, I tried going, but as we were doing yoga one day, I was repulsed by the mats that were used repeatedly and refused to do it.

One day, they pulled me aside and let me know that they felt like I was ready for half days, so for a week I started leaving after lunch. However, a week later, they told me that insurance couldn't cover any more days, so I was being discharged. It was just as well, because I was starting to think of suicidal thoughts less and less. It seemed like many more days passed where I didn't check the box stating that I was having suicidal thoughts. Besides, I knew it was probably getting expensive, and as it turned out, I was right. Although our personal insurance covered a large chunk of my hospitalization, after the whole ordeal, we still owed thousands upon thousands of dollars. My parents have only finished paying that off recently.

Just as I was when I left inpatient care, I was terrified. Although I would still have Diane, I wouldn't have the support system that I'd had while I was in the hospital. I would have to try and use my coping skills out in the real world without any help. That prospect was terrifying, but it was inevitable.

So, out into the real world I went.

PART 5

RECOVERY

CHAPTER 1

Going back into the real world after three months in the hospital was not easy.

I had all this new information and coping skills in my head but didn't exactly have the motivation to put it in place, nor had anything clicked in my brain yet on how to do it. I desperately wanted to get better, but it just didn't seem to be happening yet.

So, after the hospital, I continued to stay in bed every day all day, hoping that the motivation would somehow come to me. This time, it was even worse because I had all of this hope of recovery inside of me but did not know how to act on it. My family and everyone else had the expectation that I would be getting better because I had just spent months in the hospital, and I felt the stress of that and didn't want to disappoint them.

But I was overwhelmed with information and didn't know how to actually put it into action. The thought of recovery was absolutely overwhelming and stressful to me.

I began to become even more dependent on Hunter, which I didn't even think was possible until it just happened. It seemed like, when I wasn't with him, a part of me was missing and I felt a huge void in my heart. I *needed* to see and talk to him every day, or I would have a full-blown panic attack. I had to hear positive validation from him on a daily basis, and all I cared about was what he thought of me and how he felt towards me. If you thought I went into rages towards him a lot before the hospital, it was 10 times worse in the months afterwards. I became more and more scared of losing him, and there were many signs that showed that.

1. Over-apologizing: I would constantly apologize for everything, even when it didn't warrant an apology. I would apologize for the smallest thing, even texting someone for no reason an apology because I thought I was annoying them.

2. Baiting for validation: I would say comments like 'nobody loves me' or 'I hate myself' to try and get my friends to say nice things about me. This made me feel better about myself and loved.

3. Doing everything for everyone: I wanted to be my friend's servant, doing everything I could possibly do for them. I thought that if I did nice things for them, they would love me more and not leave me.

4. Cause fights just to test the friendship: There were times where I wasn't mad about anything, but I would pretend to get angry and start a fight anyway. The truth is, during these situations, I wanted to see if the person would leave me. I was testing to see if they would abandon me. At times, sometimes I would even believe that negative attention was better than no attention at all.

5. Push people away: Oftentimes, I would stop talking to people and push them away from me to test them on whether they would come back. And this would just hurt the friendship.

I used all of these tactics both on Hunter and my other friends. After getting back, I continued to sleepover at Nick's house every weekend with Josh. However, Nick's relationship with me became more and more unhealthy as time went on. I craved Nick's attention. Although he wasn't my FP anymore, I still desperately wanted his approval and for him to like me. And then, somehow, two years after our first hook up, One thing led to another and somehow, we were back there, but this time, we both wanted it.

Meanwhile, my rages with Hunter became more prevalent. I'd become increasingly jealous when he spent time with other people. I HATED his other friends and looked at them as a pure threat. I always believed he would start to like them better than me and that I would be replaced.

Me: *I saw you hung out with your friend John yesterday.*

Hunter: *I did, why?*

Me: *You like him better than me, don't you? Everyone always likes other people more than me. I'm everyone's last choice.*

Hunter: *That's not true, Andrew*

Me: *I should kill myself, you wouldn't care.*

Hunter: *Why would you even say that? Do I need to call the police?*

Me: *No, please don't. I'm not actually gonna do it. But even if I were to you would probably be happy*

Hunter: *I can't take this right now, I'm gonna go*

Me: *YOU HATE ME. SCREW YOU HUNTER. I'M NEVER GONNA SPEAK TO YOU AGAIN.*

Me: *I'm so sorry, I didn't mean that, please come back, don't leave me, I can't take life without you, I'm so sorry. I love you.*

Me: *Please.*

Me: *I'm begging you.*

I would then continue to text him at least a dozen times until he finally answered and told me he forgave me. After that, I would lay in bed sobbing, feeling horrible about myself and what I just did. I would often feel suicidal after these outbursts.

It wasn't long before I realized that alcohol masked the pain and anxiety that I so strongly felt all of the time. So, I started to drink more and more, getting drunker and drunker every time. Although I would tell myself I'm never going to drink again after each time, I would then talk myself into drinking again and again. Just one more.

There was one time that summer after my hospitalization that I went to a hotel party at a conference in Washington DC. Each drink I made, I poured myself half vodka and half lemonade, just wanting to get plastered because it felt so good. I felt so free when I was drunk, because it was one of the few times I didn't care about anything. I ended up blacking out and embarrassing myself in front of some of the most important people in the animal rights movement, probably hurting my chance at a career at any of the nonprofits represented there. My friends and my boss in my internship at the time ended up taking me back up to my room, where I puked all over myself and pissed my pants. They stripped me in the bathtub where I was barely conscious and not really breathing. They probably should have called an ambulance, but they didn't want to embarrass me anymore, as I'd be carried out in front of everyone at the conference. I almost drank myself to death that night, just to get rid of my anxiety. The truth was, at the time, I was hoping that I wouldn't wake up after passing out.

Another time I was alone in a house while house-sitting and decided to have a drink. One drink turned into two, and two turned into half a bottle of vodka. I woke up in bed with puke all over me, not remembering the night before. It turns out, I had thrown up on both my expensive phone and laptop, destroying them both in the process.

After a while came one of my worst drinking moments. I was spending the night at Nick's house with Josh and we decided to go up to Nick's cabin in Wisconsin. On the way there, we picked up some booze to have around the campfire. I ended up drinking so much that I was wasted. When we got back to Nick's house, stupid drunk me snuck two beers out of his fridge and chugged them alone in the bathroom. I was obliterated. First, Nick was pissed because I had stolen two beers from his parents and got drunk in his house. Second, the majority of the night, I just lay there sobbing in Nick's lap talking about how badly I wanted to kill myself. It was not a good situation.

The next morning, out of guilt, I went out and bought them their favorite Mexican food for lunch. However, it didn't work. Even after sending them heartfelt apologies, I didn't end up hearing from them for weeks. Until Josh texted me the reason why they weren't responding. He told me that I was never a good friend and that I didn't care about any of them. Not Nick, not himself, not Charlotte. He said that I never did anything for them, and that the only person I cared about was Hunter. He said I put no effort into the friendship.

Today, I can acknowledge a lot of what they were saying. At the time, I was so wrapped up in myself and my own mental illness that it was hard to be a good friend. And many friends in the past have told me that I only cared about Hunter, and I totally understand why they think that. I focused on Hunter way too much, but it was hard for me not to when I was so dependent on him. I didn't treat all of my friends the same way I treated him and often put him above them. I can't imagine how that made them feel.

However, I'll tell you the truth. When I love, I love hard. And I loved all of them so much. With all of my heart, in fact. I cared about them more than I cared about myself and wanted to give them the world, even though I didn't have the ability to do so at the time. I wish I was able to give them the love and attention that they wanted.

So Nick, Josh, and Charlotte: if you are reading this, I am so sorry. I am sorry I did not have the capacity to treat you the way you deserved to be treated in the past years. None of you deserved that. The truth is, I was fighting so hard to survive that it was difficult to be a good friend at the time. I truly regret everything.

After they stopped being my friends, I was absolutely crushed. Just like with Emma, I felt heartbroken once again. I felt abandoned. I was hurt and angry that they had left me in my time of need. Friends are supposed to be with you during the hard times, and I felt like they did not do that for me. I felt truly alone and desperately wanted them back. And at the time, I took it as further proof that I was inherently unlovable.

I tried so hard to keep my friends, but I always seemed to just push them away.

CHAPTER 2

After losing some of my only friends at the time, it was very obvious that something needed to change and the way I was living was not working for me. It seemed as if I was never going to get the motivation to try and get better, unless I truly tried. Recovery is a choice, and from that moment on I decided to make it. So I decided to commit and give this recovery thing everything I had. My remaining friends depended on it. My future depended on it. My life depended on it.

To start off, I started going to Diane regularly. She conducted a type of therapy with me called Cognitive Behavior Therapy, or CBT.

There are a variety of distorted thoughts that run through my mind on a daily basis, and Diane tried her best to get me to reframe these into something more logical. Every session, she would teach me new ways to think about and understand my thoughts. Along with this, she taught me new coping skills. CBT focuses on changing your actions, which in turn changes your thoughts because they are both connected. Feelings are also connected and so, if you change one of them, they all can change. These are some of the thinking styles that Diane helped me to change:

1. All or nothing: Also called black or white thinking, an example of this is 'If I don't ace this test then I am stupid.'

2. Mental filter: This is where you only pay attention to certain details and ignore other evidence. For example, this may be noticing your failures but not paying attention to your successes.

3. Mind reading: In which someone assumes they know what the other person is thinking.

4. Fortune telling: Trying to predict the future.

5. Emotional reasoning: This is when one assumes that because they feel a certain way, that it must be true. For example, 'I am nervous so I must be a failure.'

6. Labeling: This is where we either assign labels t ourselves or other people. Someone may label themselves or others as ugly or a loser.

7. Overgeneralizing: Creating a pattern in your head off of one event or being too broad in the conclusions you conclude. 'Everyone always leaves me.'

8. Throwing away the positive: In which we discount good things we do or have happened to us.

9. Catastrophizing and minimizing: Making things a bigger or smaller deal than they actually are.

10. 'Should' and 'must': Saying things 'should' or 'must' be a certain way.

11. Personalization: Making things about yourself. It could also be blaming people for something that was your fault.

These are common and very unhealthy ways of thinking and I use them on a daily basis. What Diane did was teach me how to change these thoughts into something more logical. This didn't happen overnight and took a lot of practice. Diane taught me to become aware of what I was feeling, and to feel those emotions to their fullest. As a result, I was able to realize I was thinking unhealthily.

I also tried out some hospital tactics, such as grounding myself and positive self-talk. I remember looking at myself in the mirror and saying to myself, 'I am handsome. I am smart. I am worthy of love.' I may have not believed it, but the more I said it to myself the more I began to trust myself.

Having a healthier lifestyle was also extremely vital to my recovery. I started off with my sleep schedule. Instead of staying up all night and sleeping during the day, I adjusted it so that I got a solid eight hours of sleep every night. I went to bed by 11pm every night when I began my recovery process. I knew that when my sleeping schedule is messed with or I don't get enough sleep, my head doesn't work right and I go back to my old habits, becoming depressed. I discovered that it helps to make a routine, so going to bed at the same time every night helps.

Speaking of routines, eating three meals a day is also important. I was lacking various vitamins and minerals, which does affect a person's mental health. At first, I just cared about eating three meals and didn't pay attention to the healthiness of the food. But once I had that set, I began to eat healthier.

Physical exercise is very important for a person's mental health. So I started working out on my own treadmill at home and spending more time doing physical activity.

Now, there is one thing that I want to point out. I am not suggesting that a mentally ill person can just wake up one day and 'decide' to get better. It takes other things to get to that point. And those things are a good therapist and psychiatrist. You need to have a good team behind you in order to get better. It is very important not to try and do it alone. It was only after I switched over to the new medication at the hospital, and my original psychiatrist prescribed me another add-on medication that I actually started to get the motivation to reach towards recovery. It also took regular therapy to get to this point. So, for anyone who wants to recover, I suggest getting a good team behind you. I thought I could do it by myself at first too. I was wrong.

I also found it important to have a support system outside of my therapist and psychiatrist. It helps to have someone to talk to whenever you are triggered. I found that in my friends and my parents. Even if it's just one person, I would suggest finding someone you can talk to.

I learned from the hospital that control is an illusion. It's all a big myth. You can't control everything and worrying will not make a difference in something good or bad happening. You can think you have all the control in the world walking down the street but to then be hit by a bus.

I needed to realize that what I perceive in my head is not actually correct. In fact, I learned through CBT that everything in the world is neutral and has no meaning but we put our own meanings onto things. This way of thinking helps me a lot on a daily basis.

As special as everyone thinks they are, I needed to get it into my head that I am not special. The world is not against me and it is okay for me to make a mistake just like everyone else. There is nothing different about me.

These were some of the highlights of what I learned through CBT that helped transform my life. The hospital and Diane helped me to change my thoughts, actions, and feelings into something more positive. Even till this day, I am still in CBT, as it is very important to my mental health upkeep. I might not go to therapy as much, but I still make sure that I am going at least twice a month.

*

CBT was doing amazing things in my life and as always, Diane was working wonders, but when it came to my BPD, it just didn't seem to be doing or working effectively enough. BPD is sinister and targets you when you're at your weakest. It knows your biggest insecurities and takes advantage of that. It takes very specific skills to overcome BPD. For a long time, I still believed the stereotype that BPD is untreatable. That's what most people and resources say. When I was in the hospital, they had no resources for it, so I thought that not even the professionals had hope for me.

However, one day, Diane brought up a new type of therapy to me: Dialectical Behavior Therapy (DBT). According to her, this type of therapy was perfect for me. In fact, it was originally created to treat BPD.

I decided to give it a try, because I was so committed to my recovery. Diane gave me a list of places that offer it and I called the one she suggestedup. It turns out that the majority of DBT is done in group therapy. The thought of other people hearing my personal information in a therapeutic setting made me uncomfortable. At the time, I was very ashamed of my mental illness and didn't want other people knowing that information about me. However, for DBT, I was expected to share personal information about my life with a group of strangers. It scared me but it was my first time hearing that there was hope of recovery from BPD and I was so dedicated to getting better I decided to give it a try. Eventually, the day of my first DBT group started and the therapist began.

'How're we all doing today, can you all give us an update on your week?'

This was where I'd be sharing this personal information with these people for the first time. I actually felt a lot better because the group was very small. It only consisted of three other people. A man in a suit working in IT, a jolly looking preschool teacher, and a balding gym teacher. I was definitely the youngest person in the room. It was a long time until someone volunteered to share, but it seemed easy. Eventually my turn came.

'My week was alright. I've been really trying to get better lately, so I've been a lot more motivated and that feels really good. I lay in bed a good amount of the week, but pushed myself to go and work out yesterday, which seemed to help.'

I learned that day that DBT focuses on four areas. These four areas I'm about to describe are the skills that combined with medication and CBT helped me to recover.

The first skill that DBT focuses on is mindfulness. Mindfulness encourages people to accept and be present in the current moment. This skill heavily helped with my anxiety, as most of it was worrying about the future. Along with that, it helped with my depression, because it stopped me from focusing on the past. It helped me to be aware of what I was feeling and kept me grounded.

The second skill that DBT teaches is distress tolerance. This part definitely helped with my rages. It taught me that I can get through and tolerate negative emotions, instead of using negative coping skills like lashing out. Sometimes it felt like I couldn't survive when I was triggered, but the fact is I will always survive.

The third skill is emotion regulation, which also helped me with rages, but also helped me with my feelings of sadness. This skill guides the person into managing and changing overwhelming emotions. It helped me control my mood swings.

Finally, there's interpersonal effectiveness. This skill allows the person to communicate in a way that is assertive, maintains self-respect, and strengthens relationships. Learning to maintain self-respect was important to me. I was used to not having self-respect, and that is something everyone should have.

Medication, CBT, and DBT saved my life. I ended up attending DBT therapy for about a year and a half, which very much changed my life.

CHAPTER 3

For about five years, dating took a back burner. It was the last thing on my mind. On a daily basis, my thoughts were simply about surviving and on my friends. I didn't even have an urge to have a romantic relationship. Plus, I was so fixated on Nick and Hunter for the longest time, I couldn't even think about anyone else.

My anxiety and self-esteem was also a factor in me not actively looking for a partner. In my head I 'ruined everything I touched,' so I was sure that even if I were to get into a relationship, I would destroy it after some time. I was too nervous to even go after a guy, and even if I did, I would always think that I was not good enough for them or that they would look at me and see a loser. I let all of my images of myself I had in my head affect any possibility of a romantic relationship with another person.

When I look back at it, I'm glad that I didn't date for those five years. I don't believe that I could have handled a relationship or kept a healthy one. There was one thing I was right about back then: if I had a relationship, I certainly would have destroyed it fast. If I didn't destroy it, it would turn into a very unhealthy relationship. It would have been easy for me to emotionally abuse the other person and the possibilities of a very dependent relationship were huge. At the time, I always looked at myself as a loser for not ever dating anyone. However, if I were to give myself advice now to myself back then, I would have told me to wait completely and focus on your own recovery first. I would tell myself to date when I am fully able to commit to a relationship and treat the other person with respect. It sounds cliché, but it's true. You can't love another person until you learn how to love yourself.

Although I beat myself up for not dating for years, when I really committed to my recovery, I realized this and told myself I wouldn't date until I was ready. For the longest time, I did not have the capacity or the coping skills to be in a healthy relationship. So when I actually decided to commit to my recovery, I purposefully put dating on the dating at the back of my mind.

Over time, however, I became more aware of my thoughts and began to perfect my coping skills. I was getting better day by day, and slowly but surely my friendships were becoming healthier. I realized that I was so fixated on just a few friends, some of my best friends took a back burner. I was making huge progress. Now that's not to say that I didn't have moments of weakness, as I would relapse often. However, they started to occur less and happen less often. For every failure I had, eventually I would have a few wins.

I saw Amylynn and Brianna during my hardest times, but I think I took them for granted and didn't give them enough attention for a few years. I am now closer to them than ever and appreciate them as I should. They are my best friends and the people I lean on the most. Truly, they care about me and are always there for me. I can always count on them after a bad day.

With my recovery, I started to become less attached to my friends and started to be able to validate myself. Although I will always be a little clingy, I'm able to have friendships now that are completely healthy. It was at this time that I realized there was one thing missing from my life that I all of a sudden really wanted: a life partner. A person to share my everyday with. With my recovery came a gaping void in me for some type of romantic relationship, a healthy one. And for the first time ever, I thought I was ready. After talking to my therapist Diane, I was only reaffirmed in that belief. She thought I was ready too. So, I decided to get started.

I found out right away in the suburbs it is very hard to meet other gay men my age. At the time, as I finally thought I was ready, I was starting at a new university, after leaving my last one, and I thought maybe I could join the pride club there. However, it was a small campus and I still had a hard time finding people. So, I downloaded every dating app I could and vowed to myself I was going to get out there and meet someone. I had always thought that online dating was for old or desperate people, but eventually I decided that it's okay and just the new way things are done. It's very common nowadays, so I decided to give it a try.

First, I downloaded Grindr. Big mistake. If you don't know what Grindr is, it's a gay hookup app. I thought that it had the most gay men on it, so it must be the best place to find someone. But it's called a hookup app for a reason. I wasn't interested in a hookup anymore, but in finding an authentic and long-term relationship. I wanted someone I really connected with. The majority of messages I got on there was from old men wanting to have sex. Yep, not my forte.

I also downloaded other apps like Bumble and OkCupid, but I found that my favorite was Tinder. Although it can also be used as a hookup app, it can really be used for whatever your intentions are. I had heard of people meeting other long-terms partners on this app, so wanted to give it a try. Right away, I thought it was a lot of fun. I would sit there in my room for hours swiping left and right on people, and getting all excited when I got a match. I also had a lot of fun talking to different people. However, it seemed like the conversations always fizzled out over time or that the guy would get creepy on me. I would also get pretty frustrated because the ones that I wanted to match with me wouldn't.

However, after a while I met someone who could actually hold a conversation and seemed pretty normal. Basically, he met the bare minimum, but I told myself I would get out there, so when he asked me out I said yes.

We met a fancy Italian restaurant, hugged, and went to our table. I was very nervous and my heart was fluttering, as it was my first date in five years, which was something I made sure not to advertise to him.

It was not a great date. He talked about himself the whole time, and whenever I tried to get a word in he would bring it right back to himself. Hey, at least the food was good and I got a free meal out of it. That's one nice thing about dating, is the free meals. Just being honest!

I really thought that date would never end, as he just kept talking and talking and I would just nod along. When dinner was finally over, he wanted to go to a Starbucks to keep talking, and of course I said yes because I have people-pleasing tendencies. The date finally ended, and I didn't want to give up, so I ended up going on two more dates with him. I won't go in to detail, as they weren't important, but I didn't feel a connection or huge attraction to him and ended up breaking up with him. It was a good try.

I went a couple of months trying to find someone who met my standards on Tinder again, until I matched with a man named Tucker. He wasn't my usual type, but despite that, I was instantly attracted to him. I was thrilled when we matched and started talking.

The first thing I noticed about Tucker was that he was really good at talking, like really good. He asked me a lot about myself. It was pretty even going back and forth about ourselves, which was a plus. The second thing was that he seemed like the sweetest guy on earth. He made me feel truly good about myself, and I was able to tell right away that he was just a really good person.

I could tell that when we talked, he really cared about everything I said and truly wanted to get to know me.

We had so much in common, even Diane warned me that it might be too good to be true. We both hadn't dated since high school, wanted the same things, and were both activists. He was really passionate about social justice issues and had lived in Southern Illinois for a year mentoring underprivileged kids. He told me that he had high ambitions and wanted to be a lawyer one day.

Our conversation flowed freely and without effort. It all just felt natural and right. We eventually exchanged numbers and switched to text. And we continued to talk all day every day for months. We decided not to meet in person until we really got to know each other, as I think we were both kind of hesitant because we both hadn't really dated for a long time. Eventually, he asked me out and I was so happy. Although I hadn't met him in person yet, I really liked him and wanted it to go well. I just knew that he was relationship material and knew that we could have a future. I knew that even before we met, so there was a lot of pressure. All I knew is that I didn't want my mental health to ruin this.

We met for the first time at another Italian restaurant and winery, as we both love wine. And just like my date with Daniel, my first ever boyfriend, five years prior, we sat there for hours and just talked. We may have been texting for months, but we didn't have any awkward pauses in real life and everything just felt like it settled in place. We connected in a very profound way and my attraction to him just amplified. I knew right then and there that he would be someone who would end up being very important in my life.

It turns out that Tucker is the amazing person I thought he was. He is incredibly kind, passionate, driven, and caring. When he loves someone, he truly cares about them and he shows it. He is the sweetest and most caring person I've ever met. He wants the best for everyone.

We went on one date, which turned into two, which turned into four, until I lost count. It was all very passionate and intense, and we just wanted to be with each other all the time. However, it was a sharp contrast to my past relationships with other guys. It was pretty healthy. I didn't feel the need to try and control him. I didn't get constantly jealous or start fights. I didn't turn him into a new FP. Today, I can say that he is my favorite person in the world and my best friend, but not the kind of FP I had before. I have to work every day not to change him into an unhealthy FP, as I always have those tendencies. I have reached the point where I know the coping mechanisms to be in a healthy relationship and am able to hold one down. A year later, we are still together and stronger than ever. I can't predict what our future holds, but all I know is that he changed my life for the better and makes me a better person every-day. I know I love him. Truly.

My entire life, I had viewed love in a very unique way. I know now that until I met Tucker, I didn't know what true love actually was. My mental illness had lied to me and gave me a wrong idea of what it is. Love for me was always putting someone up on a pedestal. It was looking at a person as perfect with no flaws. It was doing anything for another person, even to your own detriment. I thought when you loved someone, you needed each other's validation constantly and spend all of your time with them.

Through my relationship with Tucker, I have learned what real love is. What I thought was love, was not love. It was idealization. It was obsession. I know now that I was never in love with Nick or Hunter. It was my BPD making them my life. It was my mental illness lying to me. I can fully say now that until I met my current partner, I had never actually been in love. What I felt before might have manifested as my head as love, but it was not. It was mere obsession.

Love is an equal partnership. Love is knowing that your significant other isn't perfect but loving them anyway. Love is recognizing each other's flaws and working on them together.

Love is communicating when you solve problems and not controlling the other person. Love is without judgement or hate.

I'm here to tell you now that although many people with BPD feel like they can never find love, they can. Despite the stereotypes, it is possible for someone with BPD to have a healthy relationship and love someone purely. I am here to tell you that BPD can be controlled, despite what the misconceptions are. You can love. You can be loved. You are loveable. And you deserve love.

CHAPTER 4

Since committing to my recovery, getting on the right medication, and going through the various therapies, I am thrilled to say that I am now living a happy, fulling life. I no longer live in bed.

My passion is back and I have gotten into animal rights activism again, doing an internship at a nonprofit and attending frequent events. Although I am not as active as I used to be, it's nice to be passionate about something again.

Through my own personal experiences, I've also become extremely passionate about mental health issues and it's become my main passion. I plan to make it my life's goal to make more resources accessible for those suffering with BPD, because there's simply not enough out there. I also want to help break the stigma that always comes with mental illness and encourage people to seek help instead of staying silent. The fact is, mental illness is nothing to be ashamed of. I was always angry I had mental illness and asked *Why me?*. But the fact is, I know why I have mental illness now. I suffered so that I can use my experiences to help other people.

Alcohol-wise, as my depression improved, my drinking problem did as well. I no longer regularly binge-drink, and only drink periodically. I've realized the impact alcohol has on me and my relationships, and I don't want that anymore. I don't want to do anything that worsens my mental health. In fact, I eat regularly now and go to the gym as much as I can. Although I was so skinny before, I am now trying to lose my belly. Let's just say that compared to the 105 pounds I weighed last year, I now weigh almost 160. In fact, I have stretch marks from gaining so much weight so fast. Hopefully soon I'll have washboard abs! The world can only hope.

I am closer to my family than ever, despite how much I pushed them away while suffering. My sister Megan and I are best friends and not a day goes by that we don't get closer. Aidan and I have a good relationship. I've bonded more with my parents and spend more time with them than ever.

I am back in school studying creative writing. It was through writing this book that I re-found my passion of writing and storytelling. Writing is my passion now, and I want to do it for the rest of my life. Through my writing, I hope to write mental-health related stories. I have already started my first fiction book.

Whereas I wasn't able to hold a job in past years, I am now holding a job teaching kids English and writing.

Although for years I haven't been able to handle a relationship, that has changed as well. I am still in a healthy relationship with Tucker. I am not dependent on him, and although I still love some positive attention and validation, I do not beg for it. I am not jealous or needy. That feels amazing.

Remember Emma, my first ever abandonment? A couple of summers ago she messaged me with an apology. Although I do not think we will ever be close again, that felt amazing and I hope to get coffee with her soon. I am glad to know she's doing well and progressing in her life, and it was good to get some final closure.

I am still not friends with Nick, Josh, and Charlotte. But that's okay and I have accepted it and moved on. I have stopped begging them to come back. I do wish they would get to know the new me, but I know now that's their loss. I have some amazing friends and my chosen 'sibs,' Amylynn and Brianna.

I am not close with Hunter anymore. He is there for me and I am there for him, and it will always be that way. I still get triggered a lot when it comes to him, but I am able to control myself and my reactions more. We plan on keeping up with each other, as we still do care about each other.

Now, this is not to say that I am not still recovering. I will always be recovering, and I always need to watch myself. At times, I am still a mess. At times, I still spend days in my bed and lay there crying for hours. I still go into rages. But they are more faw and fer between. I will be the first to admit that yes, I still do have suicidal thoughts once in a while. However, now I know that a thought is just a thought and I am able to change them. Although I will always be mentally ill, I now have the skills I need to know in order to survive. I relapse every now and again, but instead of kicking myself for it like I used to, I now pick myself up and carry on. I know now how to do that. I am a survivor. And I'm darn proud of it.

ACKNOWLEDGMENTS

Writing a book has been a dream of mine for as long as I could remember, and I first have to thank everyone at Trigger Publishing for believing in me and publishing my book. Thank you for all of your support, taking a chance on me, and making my dream come to fruition. In particular, I would like to sincerely thank my editor Kasim for all of the work he did and the patience he had with me. I know I wasn't always easy to work with, so I appreciate everything. I thank you for making this process so amazing!

Thank you to Jason for giving me the original idea for this book and for constantly helping me become a better version of myself. You have made a huge difference in my life, more than you will ever know. Thank you for being a constant source of inspiration for me and loving me no matter what. You are onto big things.

Thank you Grandma Mary for being one of my biggest supporters, understanding me like no other, and always being there for me. You have no idea the positive impact you have on my life.

Megan, thank you for always supporting me no matter what and being one of my closest friends. I know I can always count on you. I love you.

Thank you to Diane for always believing in me and for being there for me all of these years. You are the reason I am still here, and for that I will be forever grateful.

Amylynn and Brianna, thank you for always being there for me and for being people I could always count on. You will always be my 'sibs.'

Tucker, you are my world and the love of my life. You are responsible for teaching me what true love is. I am a better person because of you, and I thank God every day for putting you in my life. Thank you from the bottom of my heart from being there for me through my highs and lows, constantly supporting me, reading through the many drafts and catching my typos, and just being 'my person.' I love you so much. Life with you is a constant adventure.

And finally, the biggest thank you to my parents, who I consider the best parents in the world. Thank you for being my rock, always pushing me to be better, and sticking by my side even when I don't deserve it. You both mean the world to me and I love you two so much.

REFERENCES

1. **Gray, P. (2014).** *The Danger of Back to School*. Retrieved from https://www.psychologytoday.com/us/blog/freedom-learn/201408/the-danger-back-school.
[accessed 15.04.2019]

**If you found this book interesting ...
why not read these next?**

Man Up Man Down

Standing up to Suicide

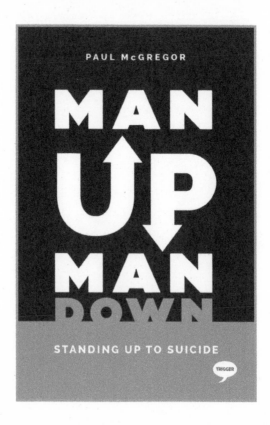

When his dad died suddenly by suicide, Paul was devastated.
Now he's on a mission to change how we think about men's
mental health and what it really means to "man up".

Beautiful Chaos

A Life Worth Living with Bipolar

On the outside, TV news anchor and sports presenter
Ali Douglas lived a glamourous, showbiz lifestyle.
But secretly, she was battling terrible mood swings and
crushing depression. The diagnosis Ali received after
35 years of waiting would change her life forever ...

Walk a Mile

Anxiety in a Professional World

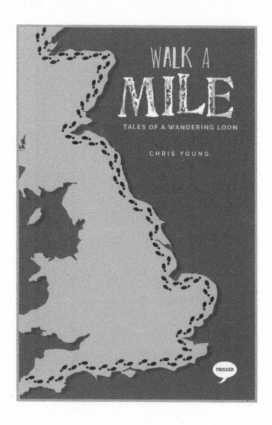

This is the story of Chris Young, a sufferer of BPD, who decided to walk around the edge of the UK, challenging mental health stigma one conversation at a time.

the *Shaw* **mind**
FOUNDATION

Creating hope for children,
adults and families

Sign up to our charity, The Shaw Mind Foundation

www.shawmindfoundation.org

and keep in touch with us; we would love to hear
from you.

*We aim to bring to an end the suffering and despair caused
by mental health issues. Our goal is to make help and support
available for every single person in society, from all walks of
life. We will never stop offering hope. These are our promises.*

TRIGGER™

The mental health & wellbeing publisher

www.triggerpublishing.com

Trigger is a publishing house devoted to opening conversations about mental health. We tell the stories of people who have suffered from mental illnesses and recovered, so that others may learn from them.

Adam Shaw is a worldwide mental health advocate and philanthropist. Now in recovery from mental health issues, he is committed to helping others suffering from debilitating mental health issues through the global charity he co-founded, The Shaw Mind Foundation. www.shawmindfoundation.org

Lauren Callaghan (CPsychol, PGDipClinPsych, PgCert, MA (hons), LLB (hons), BA), born and educated in New Zealand, is an innovative industry-leading psychologist based in London, United Kingdom. Lauren has worked with children and young people, and their families, in a number of clinical settings providing evidence based treatments for a range of illnesses, including anxiety and obsessional problems. She was a psychologist at the specialist national treatment centres for severe obsessional problems in the UK and is renowned as an expert in the field of mental health, recognised for diagnosing and successfully treating OCD and anxiety related illnesses in particular. In addition to appearing as a treating clinician in the critically acclaimed and BAFTA award-winning documentary *Bedlam*, Lauren is a frequent guest speaker on mental health conditions in the media and at academic conferences. Lauren also acts as a guest lecturer and honorary researcher at the Institute of Psychiatry Kings College, UCL.